AMERICAN
LANDSCAPE
ARCHITECTURE

DESIGNERS AND PLACES

AMERICAN LANDSCAPE ARCHITECTURE

DESIGNERS AND PLACES

Building Watchers Series

NATIONAL TRUST FOR HISTORIC PRESERVATION
AMERICAN SOCIETY OF LANDSCAPE ARCHITECTS

THE PRESERVATION PRESS

The Preservation Press
National Trust for Historic Preservation
1785 Massachusetts Avenue, N.W.
Washington, D.C. 20036

The National Trust for Historic Preservation in the United
States is the only private, nonprofit organization chartered by
Congress to encourage public participation in the preservation
of sites, buildings and objects significant in American history
and culture. Support is provided by membership dues, endowment funds, contributions and grants from federal agencies, including the U.S. Department of the Interior, under provisions
of the National Historic Preservation Act of 1966. The opinions
expressed herein do not necessarily reflect the views or policies
of the Interior Department. For information about membership
in the National Trust, write to the above address.

Dedicated to the memory of my father, William John Tishler, a
skillful builder, and my mother, Mary Sarter Tishler, an avid
gardener.

William H. Tishler wishes to thank the following persons for
their special assistance with this book: Arnold R. Alanen, Barry
Buxton, Leslie Rose Close, Sally Domini, Carol Doty, Pat
Filzen, Raymond L. Freeman, Mara Gelbloom, Robert E. Grese,
Kenneth I. Helphand, Catherine M. Howett, Daniel W. Krall,
Richard Longstreth, Miriam Easton Rutz, John R. Stilgoe, Betsy
L. Tishler, Dell Upton, Michael Van Valkenburgh, Christopher
Vernon and Cynthia Zaitzevsky.

Printed in the United States of America
96 95 94 93 92 91 90 89 5 4 3 2 1

Library of Congress Cataloging in Publication Data

American landscape architecture : designers and places / edited
    by William H. Tishler.
        p.   cm.   — (Building watchers series)
        Bibliography: p.
        Includes index.
        ISBN 0-89133-145-X (pbk.) : $10.95
        1. Landscape architecture—United States—History.
    2. Landscape architects—United States—History.   3. Landscape
    architects—United States—Biography.   I. Tishler, William H.
    II. Series.
    SB470.53.A44 1989
    712′ .0973—dc19   88-19632

Published in cooperation with the American Society of Landscape Architects

Edited by Diane Maddex, director, and Janet Walker, managing
editor, The Preservation Press

Designed by Anne Masters, Washington, D.C.

Composed in Trump Mediaeval by BG Composition, Inc.,
Baltimore, Md.

Printed on 70-pound Frostbrite by Science Press, Ephrata, Pa.

Contents

Foreword

Central Park in New York City. The Blue Ridge Parkway winding through Virginia and North Carolina. These places are two of the best-known designed landscapes in America.

What is not generally known is the challenge these sites posed to their designers. In what is now Central Park was a blocks-long rubble pile. Where the Blue Ridge Parkway today skirts the mountain tops were eroded mountain lands, cut-over forests and commercialized "scenic" areas. What exists now—even years after their work was completed—is so perfectly executed as to belie the genius of the design, the vision of the landscape architects and the work of collaborating professions and trades that made these projects possible.

These and many other sites detailed in this book have become favorite places for people to gather, to enjoy both actively and passively, to be "in nature"—that is, in natural settings shaped by landscape architects.

As with the great plazas and gardens of the Old World, other designed landscapes in America have paid less homage to nature and more attention to the joy of created space. Landscape architects have designed countless urban plazas, squares and public spaces that, while obviously designed, are indeed places for people.

Regardless of whether the ultimate landscape design is natural or created, perhaps the most interesting aspect of landscape architecture today is its diversity: the various sciences that are brought together, the arts, the variety of "hard" paving and structural materials and "soft" materials such as water and plants, the differing scales of the palettes on which landscape architects work. This diversity ranges from planning for regions and ecosystems to designing a vest-pocket park that enriches an urban scene. Landscape architects are trained to manage and coordinate projects that cross professional lines from infrastructure to architecture and engineering, sociology to the fine arts, irrigation to horticulture and biology.

As you are about to read, the broad scope of the profession is clearly reflected in the practice of Frederick Law Olmsted. Father of American landscape architecture, Olmsted carried on a diversified practice, including parks ranging from Yosemite in California to Boston's urban system, as well as new towns and estates. And the variety of disciplines Olmsted used foreshadowed what the profession as a whole was to become.

The timelessness of the designs of Olmsted and the other landscape architects detailed in this book and the evolution of landscape architecture in America can be seen today because of efforts by countless concerned parties, from local community groups to national organizations such as the National Trust for Historic Preservation. The American Society of Landscape Architects salutes the National Trust for undertaking the publication of this book and highlighting this exciting profession.

Brian S. Kubota, FASLA
President
American Society
of Landscape Architects

Introduction

Since the dawn of civilization on this continent, a bountiful landscape has attracted people to America. Long before the arrival of Europeans, Native Americans fostered a gentle stewardship of the land. Then, a young nation's growing population began exploiting the seemingly limitless resources. Cutting, plowing, draining, filling and building resulted in a dramatic transformation of the American environment. It would be 200 years before visionaries came forth to advocate the systematic design of outdoor space as an integral component of this emerging landscape. Embracing both art and science, their work kindled the fledgling profession of landscape architecture. *American Landscape Architecture: Designers and Places* is a tribute to these individuals and the remarkable accomplishments of the young and dynamic profession they initiated.

Inspired by new democratic ideals and growing social concerns, early landscape designers combined agricultural methods, civil engineering techniques and artistic principles to shape the land. Their work reflected a quest for beauty and function combined with responsible land stewardship. An astute amateur gardener, Thomas Jefferson in 1805 regarded this activity as one of the fine arts: "not horticulture but the art of embellishing grounds by fancy." Jefferson's concepts, as noted in William L. Beiswanger's essay, would shape landscapes not only for dwellings and agrarian activities, but also for educational environments, entire towns and the young democracy's vast western countryside. Others from horticultural and landscape gardening backgrounds—including André Parmentier, Andrew Jackson Downing, Adolph Strauch, Jacob Weidenmann and Robert Morris Copeland—expanded the early foundations of landscape architecture in America. The most influential and inventive of these was Downing. Had he not died in a tragic accident at the age of 36, the development of landscape architecture in this country would undoubtedly have been accelerated and the profession's legacy would be even richer.

Frederick Law Olmsted, assisted by his partner Calvert Vaux, became the acknowledged father of American landscape architecture. A farsighted genius whose accomplishments in his field remain unparalleled to this day, Olmsted's prolific career legitimized the design of outdoor space as a profession. As Olmsted scholar Charles E. Beveridge notes, he "provided his fellow citizens with recreational and residential amenities that had previously been monopolized by the privileged classes of Europe." Inspired by Downing, his mentor, Olmsted's vision established the lofty ideals that will forever guide the profession's underlying philosophy.

A pioneering landscape architect with a career remarkably similar to Olmsted's was his longtime friend H. W. S. Cleveland. A brilliant idealist, Cleveland carried the eastern traditions of landscape architecture westward with the expanding American frontier. During his nearly 50-year career, Cleveland became an enlightening spokesman for his new profession. The designer of a wide range of projects, he was one of the earliest advocates for conserving large interconnected systems of open space and landscape amenities from "the vandalism which is the inevitable companion of civilization." His work has only recently begun to receive the recognition it rightly deserves.

Jacob Weidenmann, like Parmentier and Strauch, another pre–Civil War practitioner, received training in Europe before emigrating to the United States. Influenced by Downing's writings and his brief employment with Olmsted and Vaux, Weidenmann established an active office in Connecticut. Then, like Cleveland, he moved to Chicago to seek new opportunities in the burgeoning Midwest. However, discouraged by his unsuccessful efforts there, Weidenmann returned to New York City to continue his fascination with what he considered the "noblest of all Art professions."

With its beginnings secured, a small but important group of landscape architects emerged to lead the profession into the 20th century. Some of the most significant of these—John Charles Olmsted, Charles Eliot, Warren H. Manning and Frederick Law Olmsted, Jr.—had apprenticed with the senior Olmsted. Others, such as Jens Jensen,

Charles A. Platt, Frank Waugh and Ellen Biddle Shipman, took different paths to enter the profession. Appropriately, Frederick Law Olmsted lived to see his influence help establish formal education for the profession. Shortly before Olmsted's death, his son Frederick developed the nation's first landscape architectural curriculum at Harvard University in 1900. This program produced most of America's leading landscape architects for the next half century, including such distinguished early graduates as Henry Vincent Hubbard, Elbert Peets and Thomas Church.

As in the other professions, women pursuing a career in landscape design once lacked access to the traditional educational and career opportunities available to their male counterparts. Fortunately, the role of early women practitioners is becoming better understood and is now an important aspect of landscape architectural history. The inspiring careers of Ellen Biddle Shipman and Beatrix Jones Farrand serve to illustrate the significant contributions women have made to the history of American landscape architecture.

With the midpoint of its second century of activity approaching, the practice of landscape architecture in America can be associated with an overwhelming series of accomplishments. Many are highlighted in the places and subjects of *American Landscape Architecture*—natural and built surroundings that permeate the very essence of American society to enrich our quality of life. These places range from environments designed to satisfy basic living, recreational and utilitarian needs to bold projects advocated by the large number of visionaries who have always been attracted to the profession.

Defining and organizing such a panorama of activities pose a sizable challenge. To balance the 21 distinguished early professionals profiled in the first section of this book, 21 place types were selected and are discussed in alphabetical order. They represent land-shaping activities that occurred during four general time periods in the development of American landscape architecture: (1) early American beginnings; (2) 1850 to 1900, a period that witnessed the emergence of the profession; (3) 1900 to 1950, an era of expansion and growing opportunities in the public sector; and (4) 1960 to the present, a time of new ecological insights and technological opportunities. Unlike buildings, which can be constructed in a relatively short period of time, landscape designs may take more than a few years to complete and to mature to achieve the designer's intended effect. Dates for sites given in these essays provide a general historical framework and cannot always represent the precise initiation and completion dates; unless otherwise specified, dates indicate years in which active work was started, conducted or completed.

During the early preprofessional era of projects included in this book, places emerged that represent America's first attempts to shape traditional forms of outdoor space. The garden—that timeless manifestation of landscape design found in the most ancient civilizations—became America's earliest form of landscape design. It was slow in taking hold, however, because of the more serious preoccupation with creating a new world out of the continent's formidable wilderness—itself a form of nature's vast garden. The first primitive gardens developed as unconscious design expressions and were an outgrowth of utilitarian food production needs. Later, where wealth and conditions permitted, formal gardens were built—symbols of mastering a yet untamed world. Cemeteries represented early attempts at laying out functional and attractive outdoor spaces on a somewhat more grandiose scale. Here the task called for defined plots of green, access and ornamentation with plants and other landscape features. Early in the 19th century the proliferation of country estates provided new opportunities for landscape designers. Many prominent gardeners, horticulturists and other "rural embellishers" were active in laying out their opulent grounds. Andrew Jackson Downing adapted the picturesque aesthetic to these handsome villas and set new levels of taste for this traditional landscape expression. With the need to provide a more public form of access to groups of academic buildings, campus design offered opportunities for shaping new forms of outdoor space. Today, college campuses demonstrate a wide diversity of landscape design, and many still retain important examples of work by early landscape architects.

As landscape architecture evolved into a more established profession in the latter half of the 19th century, new forms of designed landscapes emerged on the American scene. Of these, urban parks became one of the most popular and influential. While versions of the park concept had been a feature of European landscapes for some time, America's first public example was the green expanse of pasture we know today as the Boston Common. The genius of Frederick Law Olmsted was crucial in sparking America's urban park movement. This extraordinary parkmaker's innovative design and subsequent implementation of the plan for Central Park stand, to this day, as one of the profession's most outstanding achievements. Closely related to the development of urban parks was the concept of vast networks of open space connecting landscape features in and around large cities. Incorporating outlying areas of greenery with major water features, boulevards and inner-city parks, metropolitan open space systems represented grand planning strategies and a bold new scale of thinking. Later they would become a hallmark of progressive landscape architects and a central element in large-scale landscape and ecological planning.

With the growing availability of leisure time, the landscape became central to the recreational experiences of many Americans. Landscape architects have traditionally been involved with the planning and development of such recreational areas. While gardens, cemeteries and parks of all kinds provided early recreational opportunities, other facilities including amusement parks, camps, clubs, golf courses, resorts, spas and zoos evolved to serve the growing population's needs. Planning larger housing environments also emerged under the guise of landscape architecture. Olmsted and Vaux's plan for Riverside, Ill., became an innovative early example of the romantic suburb—a blend of access to city opportunities with pleasures of the countryside. Later, large public housing projects incorporated superblocks designed to include a nucleus of green space while accommodating limited automobile access.

The beginning of the 20th century brought exciting new challenges and opportunities to what was still a fledgling profession. Two major achievements launched the profession into this era. In 1899 the American Society of Landscape Architects was founded. The following year formal instruction in landscape architecture began at Harvard, the nation's most prestigious university. Always comfortable in a collaborative role, landscape architects became leaders in establishing what would become the separate and highly interdisciplinary profession of city planning—a profession that would claim as its adherents many who would otherwise have turned to landscape architecture. Some argued later that the severance of this important activity from the profession of landscape architecture occurred because the profession had been preoccupied with less socially conscious, but more lucrative, commissions offered by the golden era of estate design that flourished until the Depression.

That turning point in American history—the Depression—brought difficult times for many private offices run by landscape architects, but it also opened new horizons in public practice with opportunities afforded by a host of New Deal programs. The resulting flurry of public works activity required professionals with an array of skills in planning, site development, construction implementation and resource management. The landscape architect was ideally suited for these tasks. Soon, a new wave of public practitioners emerged to meet this challenge from the increasing number of academic landscape architectural programs. Their leadership and skill were demonstrated clearly in the development of a vast system of national forests as well as state and national parks that remain unparalleled anywhere in the world. Of particular interest was the role the elder Frederick Law Olmsted, and later his son Frederick, played in shaping America's national park policy. The senior Olmsted, with his typical futuristic outlook, planted the seeds for a visionary system of national parks in his work for the Commission on the Yosemite Valley in the 1860s. Following in his father's footsteps, the younger Olmsted developed a lifelong interest in conservation that resulted in a remarkable series of achievements advocating state and national park planning.

During the early years of the 20th century, the parkway also emerged as an accepted landscape feature. Precursors for such systems were envisioned earlier by the senior Olmsted, Cleveland and others (even William Penn, as Harley E. Jolley notes in his essay, is thought to have incorporated a parkway into his beloved Philadelphia). However, the parkway phenomenon as we know it today became a reality with the advent of the automobile, first reaching fruition with the Blue Ridge Highway in 1909. Planning entire communities was also an important activity that emerged during this period. Based on earlier precedents that included New England mill towns, planned suburbs, corporate model villages and the garden cities of England, these complex developments reached their zenith in the greenbelt towns of the 1930s. Again, landscape architects played a key role in designing many of these communities.

The remaining place-related topics in this book emerged and flourished in the American landscape, for the most part, after World War II. Today, attractive businesses and industries can be found in both urban settings and parklike suburban locations as corporate America uses the landscape in its imagery and symbolism. Designs for new urban spaces that include squares and plazas are injecting new vitality into our cities. Along our community waterfronts an array of projects have brought people into new and stimulating relationships with this lifeline. Many derelict buildings and obsolete industrial areas along these waterfronts have been revitalized through preservation and adaptive use.

But the concept of historic preservation has grown beyond the confines of architecture to include the landscape itself. Now the preservation of comprehensive districts, neighborhoods, communities and entire rural landscapes has captured the attention of landscape architects, and our heritage is richer because of it. Similar in spirit and ethic to conserving historic landscapes has been the recent interest in restoring disturbed sites to their earlier natural character. Ugly quarries, strip-mined areas and other disfigured landscapes are being made productive and enjoyable again thanks to new revegetation concepts and other resource management techniques.

One of the most noteworthy advancements of landscape architecture in recent times has occurred in large-scale landscape planning. Thanks to an infusion of ecological values and new technology, members of the profession assumed important leadership roles in this vital land stewardship activity. A significant contribution to managing wild and rural landscapes has been the development of techniques for assessing and protecting scenic quality. A cherished national resource, our landscape scenery can now be better protected with a variety of programs that emerged from methods pioneered mainly by U.S. Forest Service landscape architects.

In providing an introduction to several centuries of the landscape tradition in America, *American Landscape Architecture* highlights an extraordinary series of accomplishments. It portrays the careers of the eminent visionaries who launched a profession in their call for shaping environments with creativity and sensitivity toward nature.

Thousands now follow this calling. More than 60 programs in landscape architecture exist at American colleges and universities, forming an education system in this field unparalleled anywhere in the world. Innovative research is beginning to provide vital new knowledge for the practitioner. Today, the field of landscape architecture has matured and is expanding into new and exciting horizons. It has been said that the profession has reached the point where it now has the ability to invent its own future.

In the course of its relatively young history, this nation has changed the face of a vast continent. Far too much development, however, has created a formless and grotesque travesty that has changed forever the splendors of much of the pre-settlement landscape. Yet an ethic for shaping our land has also emerged, and we can claim a remarkable array of outdoor spaces that enrich the human spirit and add immeasurably to our quality of life. Combined with the people and places mentioned in this book, this ethic has become an integral part of our country's landscape architectural heritage. A better understanding of this legacy can help us shape future environments that will continue, and perhaps even strengthen, the inseparable relationship Americans have always had with their land.

William H. Tishler, ASLA

THOMAS JEFFERSON
William L. Beiswanger

Thomas Jefferson (1743–1826) regarded landscape gardening as a fine art particularly appropriate for study by Americans, for he believed that in this country "the noblest gardens may be made without expense. We have only to cut
out the superabundant plants." He brought to this art his
keen interest in the natural world (expressed in his book
Notes on the State of Virginia) and an appreciation of English theories of garden design.

His earliest thoughts on the subject of landscape design
are found in his 1771 memorandum book, in which he re-
corded ideas for the improvement of the grounds at Monticello (1768–1809), his Charlottesville, Va., estate. These
ideas, among the first mature thoughts in America on the
English or "natural" style of landscape gardening, are derived from the readings of the English poets Alexander
Pope and William Shenstone, as well as Lord Kames and
Thomas Whately, among others. Whately's treatise *Obser-
vations on Modern Gardening* (1770) served as Jefferson's
guide when he and another future president, John Adams,
toured the gardens of England in 1786. He discovered that
"the gardening in that country is the article in which it sur-
passes all the earth," but for Virginia, where "shade is our
Elysium," he proposed an American equivalent. For the
English "canvas" of open ground, "variegated with clumps
of trees distributed with taste," he substituted a grove of
shade trees "of the loftiest stature" planted with their tops
united and limbs pruned "as high as the constitution and
form of the tree will bear." Where the English had clumps
of trees on lawns, he envisioned thickets of native shrubs
under the forest canopy.

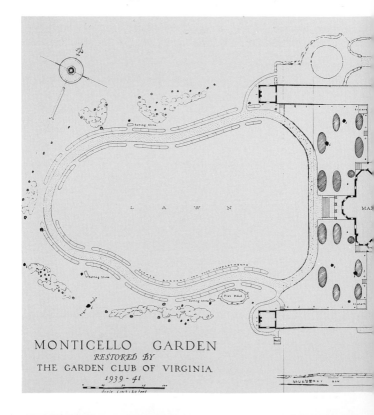

MONTICELLO GARDEN
RESTORED BY
THE GARDEN CLUB OF VIRGINIA
1939 – 41

Thomas Jefferson, by Gilbert Stuart, 1805. (Thomas Jefferson Memorial Foundation; National Portrait Gallery, Smithsonian Institution)

West front and gardens, Monticello. (James Tkatch, Thomas Jefferson Memorial Foundation)

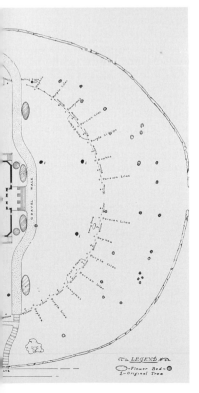

Plan for the gardens adjacent to the house at Monticello, based on Jefferson's drawings and notes, c. 1808. Ovals indicate flowers or shrubs. (Thomas Jefferson Memorial Foundation)

Walkway at Monticello, extending the house into the landscape.
(H. Andrew Johnson, Thomas Jefferson Memorial Foundation)

When Jefferson returned from a five-year diplomatic mission to France in 1789, he introduced at Monticello the English concept of the ornamental farm where the "attributes of a garden" were interspersed among the plantation-associated "articles of husbandry," such as areas for livestock and crops. In a sense Jefferson was demonstrating how a nation of farmers could live in a setting uniting utility and profit with beauty and pleasure. These theories, however, were not widely known beyond a circle of friends.

It may seem surprising, given Jefferson's love of the natural or irregular landscape, that he was instrumental in writing the Land Ordinance of 1784, which projected a gridiron imprint on the land beyond the Appalachians. In part, the grid can be explained by the country's interest in quickly settling a vast unexplored part of the continent. But Jefferson's preference for this form is evident again in a proposal made while president for "chequer board" towns with buildings constructed on the black squares and the white ones "left open, in turf and trees." Every house would front an open square, and "the atmosphere of such a town," he wrote in 1805, "would be like that of the country." In 1804 he proposed that New Orleans be extended on such a plan, arguing that it would help prevent the outbreak of yellow fever. Although not adopted there, it was implemented in modified form in Jeffersonville, Ind. (1802), and Jackson, Miss. (1821), but subsequent changes obliterated traces of the original pattern in both cities.

Jefferson's last major project was the creation of the University of Virginia in Charlottesville (1817–26). He conceived of it as an "academical village" of buildings and open spaces unified by colonnades, arcades and serpentine walls. There, in his greatest achievement as a designer of the environment, he brought together his ideas on architecture, town planning and landscape design to create what many consider the most beautiful outdoor room in America. 🖋

Opposite: Design for an observation tower, 1770s. The tower, never built, was meant to sit on top of Montalto, a small mountain facing Monticello. (Massachusetts Historical Society)

Montalto, from the gardens at Monticello. (H. Andrew Johnson, Thomas Jefferson Memorial Foundation)

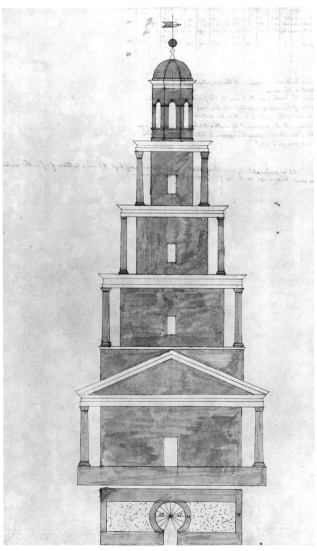

Portion of the ornamental farm planned for the hillside below Monticello, 1790s. (Henry E. Huntington Library and Art Gallery)

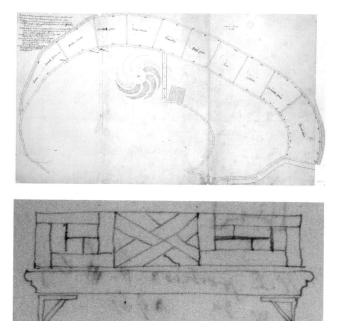

Jefferson's design for a Chinese lattice bench. (Massachusetts Historical Society)

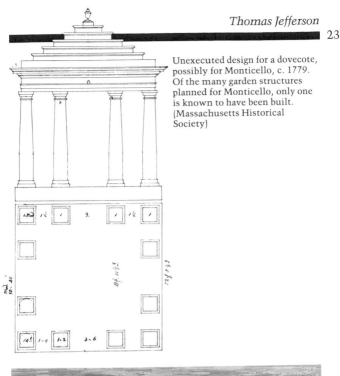

Unexecuted design for a dovecote, possibly for Monticello, c. 1779. Of the many garden structures planned for Monticello, only one is known to have been built. (Massachusetts Historical Society)

North-central Wisconsin landscape reflecting the gridiron pattern advocated by Jefferson for land division. (B-Wolfgang Hoffmann)

University of Virginia, 1856. The central terraced lawn has been called the most beautiful outdoor room in America. (C. Bohn; University of Virginia Library)

H. W. S. CLEVELAND
William H. Tishler

In 1835 H. W. S. Cleveland (1814–1900) ventured into America's heartland and found a "vast, virtually unsettled frontier." Later, he returned to the Midwest with a prophetic call for order and beauty as turbulent development swept through the area. By the end of the century, this remarkable landscape architect's achievements in the region became the highlights of a prolific career that extended from Minnesota to Georgia and from Nova Scotia to Kansas.

Born in Lancaster, Mass., into a New England maritime family, Cleveland worked at surveying before turning to farming in New Jersey. Through his activities with the National Pomological Congress he met Andrew Jackson Downing, who sparked Cleveland's growing interest in landscape design. In 1854 he returned to Massachusetts to practice "landscape and ornamental gardening," at first in association with Robert Morris Copeland. Encouraged by the demand for their expertise, they entered the competition to design Central Park but lost to Frederick Law Olmsted and Calvert Vaux. Soon after, the two men parted amicably, and Cleveland extended his work into other New England states. When the Civil War lessened demand for his services, he left Massachusetts in 1867 to work in Tarrytown, N.Y., and then with Olmsted at Brooklyn's new Prospect Park, which had been designed by Vaux and Olmsted in 1865. This early association with Olmsted led to their deep mutual respect and lasting friendship.

Seeking better opportunities in the West, Cleveland moved his office to Chicago in 1869. As the booming frontier area's earliest resident landscape architect, he worked with missionary zeal to extend his young profession's ethic into western America. A skillful writer and engaging speaker, he set forth his vision for orderly growth in eloquent lectures and a variety of publications. His perceptive book, *Landscape Architecture as Applied to the Wants of the West* (1873), stressed the landscape architect's role in a region bustling with speculators, railroad construction, booming frontier towns and yeoman farmers stamping the relentless grid on the virgin prairies. Landscape architecture was, he said, the "art of arranging land so as to adapt it most conveniently, economically and gracefully to any of the varied wants of civilization."

Design for the J. Y. Scammon residence, Hyde Park, Ill., 1871. (Cleveland, "A Few Hints on Landscape Gardening in the West")

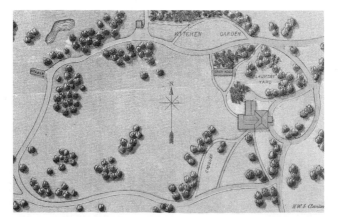

H. W. S. Cleveland, late in his
career. (Tishler collection)

Plan for Roger Williams Park, Providence, 1878, one of Cleveland's most
important projects in the East. ("Report upon the Improvement of Roger
Williams Park by the Joint Committee on Parks, with the Report of
H. W. S. Cleveland, Landscape Gardener")

Surveyors laying out the site for Milwaukee's Juneau Park, 1873, Cleveland's first project in Wisconsin. (Milwaukee Public Library)

Postcard view of Juneau Park, c. 1910, the city's first designed park. (Tishler collection)

Bethesda Springs Park, Waukesha, Wis., 1888, well known for its mineral spring water. (H. H. Bennett)

Plat map for the Jekyll Island resort, Brunswick, Ga., 1886. (Glynn County Courthouse, Brunswick)

By 1871 Cleveland had formed a loose partnership with William M. R. French, a civil engineer who later became director of the Art Institute of Chicago. Their active practice extended into nearby Wisconsin and Indiana, as well as Iowa, Minnesota, Nebraska, Kansas, Ohio and Michigan. In many of these states, Cleveland was the first landscape architect to execute projects in the name of his new profession. His pioneering work encompassed the design of cemeteries, suburbs, estates, resorts, parks, college campuses, state capitol grounds and a variety of institutional developments.

Cleveland's Chicago years were filled with tragedy, however. The great fire of 1871 devastated his office; the panic of 1873 disrupted his business; and his wife became chronically ill. The potential for implementing his bold ideas for the city diminished when his work on the South Parks (1872–76) ended in litigation for payment in 1877. In 1886, at the age of 72, he moved to Minneapolis. Rather than choose retirement there, he seized new opportunities leading to his major professional triumph and perhaps America's finest urban open space network—the Twin Cities metropolitan park system (1872–95).

In spite of extraordinary accomplishments from a distinguished career that lasted nearly half a century, Cleveland has never received proper recognition for his achievements. Yet this visionary landscape architect's legacy ranks with his profession's most significant contributions toward shaping a young nation's changing landscape. ✒

Plan for Minneapolis's 6th Ward
Park. (*Second Annual Report of
the Board of Park Commissioners
of the City of Minneapolis*, 1885)

Plan for St. Anthony Park, Minneapolis, 1873, showing topographic
features and curvilinear streets.
(Ramsey County Historical
Society)

Minnehaha Falls, c. 1910, preserved as part of the Minneapolis Park System in 1889 because of Cleveland's efforts. (Edgerton Martin collection)

Lily pond at Como Park, St. Paul, 1890. (Minnesota Historical Society)

Lake of the Isles Boulevard, Minneapolis, c. 1906, an important link in the network of parks, open spaces and parkways planned by Cleveland for the city. (Edgerton Martin collection)

Example of the "beautiful" in landscape gardening, characterized by flowing curves, soft surfaces, luxuriant vegetation and a house style in "one of the classical modes." (Downing, *Treatise*)

Example of the "picturesque," distinguished by irregular lines, abrupt and broken surfaces, a more natural and wild plant growth and rustic buildings in the Gothic, Old English and Swiss cottage styles. (*Treatise*)

Plan for the grounds of a small suburban cottage, devoted one-third to a kitchen garden, the remainder to "ornamental purposes." (Downing, *Cottage Residences*)

Andrew Jackson Downing, from a daguerreotype, c. 1850. Friends and associates often commented on Downing's ability to impress others through sheer force of personality. (George B. Tatum collection)

ANDREW JACKSON DOWNING
Catherine M. Howett

In 1845 an enthusiastic reviewer of two recent works by Andrew Jackson Downing (1815–52)—a new edition of *Treatise on the Theory and Practice of Landscape Gardening, Adapted to North America* (1841) and *Cottage Residences; or a Series of Designs for Rural Cottages, and Cottage Villas and their Gardens and Grounds* (1844)—observed that in his field of study and practice, "Mr. Downing stands, as an American, quite alone. . . . He has neither companion nor rival." Although the reviewer particularly had in mind the author's foremost position among those architects, landscape gardeners and writers who were energetically promoting the art of "rural improvement," Downing also achieved international recognition in his lifetime as a horticulturist and the most distinguished pomologist of his day; his *The Fruits and Fruit Trees of America* (1845) went through 13 editions in six years and remained the standard text throughout the century.

His management of a nursery in his hometown of Newburgh, N.Y., which he and his brother had inherited from their father, first brought Downing to the attention of the cosmopolitan circle of artists and intellectuals building country homes amid the scenic splendors of the Hudson River Valley during the opening decades of the century. As editor of the popular magazine *The Horticulturist*, he continually expanded the audience for his ideas beyond the scientific and agricultural community, beyond even the community of wealthy and well-educated clients building "first-rate villas" and estates, to those "industrious and intelligent mechanics and working men" whose humble but well-designed and well-cared-for cottages would, he believed, properly express the spirit of this country's republican institutions and family-centered morality.

If Downing was unequaled as a propagandist for the "modern" style in building and landscape design, he was nevertheless not quite alone in his enthusiasm for contemporary English models, especially the work of his friend and mentor, the prolific Scottish designer and author John Claudius Loudon. He maintained a close professional association with Alexander J. Davis and acquaintance with other American architects adapting the picturesque aesthetic to the buildings and grounds of American houses, insisting that the whole form a scenic composition rich in associations. In 1850 he brought Calvert Vaux from England

Small bracketed cottage. The bay window and vines expressed "domesticity and the presence of heart." (Downing, *The Architecture of Country Houses*, 1850)

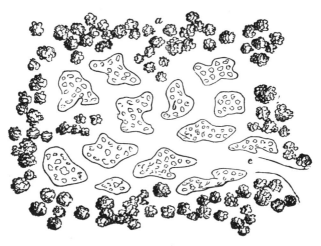

Above: Plan for an "irregular" flower garden. Downing approved of "architectural" flower gardens whose purpose was to effect a union between house and grounds. (*Treatise*)

Center: Downing's residence, near Newburgh, N.Y. He chose English Tudor for its "picturesque and striking style." (*Treatise*)

Sketch of a rustic seat, Montgomery Place, by Alexander J. Davis. Downing favored such resting places made of tree trunks and branches. (Franklin D. Roosevelt Library)

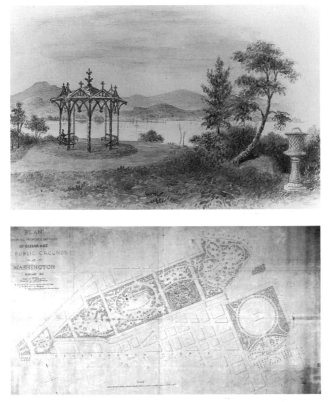

Plan for the Mall, Washington, D.C., 1851. Only a portion of Downing's plan was completed. (Geography and Maps Division, Library of Congress)

to be his partner. Others, too, would absorb, as Downing did, the influence of John Ruskin's precepts, linking the individual's capacity to appreciate nature and art—and, by extension, architecture and landscape design—to morality and the love of God.

Downing managed to simplify and codify these complex currents of thought into guidelines for action: the nature and location of the site itself should determine the choice of a particular architectural and landscape type from among those classified under the two major categories of the "beautiful" and the "picturesque"; the owner's good judgment must determine the scale of the enterprise, from modest cottage to grand villa; similarly, the choice of appropriate "embellishments," ranging from ornamental gardens to summerhouses and conservatories, must be determined by the ruling principles of "fitness," "expression of purpose" and "expression of style."

Downing's writings, more than the small number of estates he actually had a hand in designing, had a lasting impact on suburban residential design that extends even to the present day. He was an eloquent spokesman as well for the movement to create public parks and more beautiful cities. At the time of his death at 36 in a steamboat disaster, he was engaged in an ambitious plan for the design of the grounds of the United States Capitol, the White House and the Smithsonian Institution in Washington, D.C. 🪶

CALVERT VAUX
Walter L. Creese

In 1850 at the Architectural Association of London, Calvert Vaux (1824–95) was interviewed for employment by the extraordinary New York landscape gardener, Andrew Jackson Downing. Downing wanted to realign the Hudson River style of domestic architecture with the English villa-in-a-garden concept of John Claudius Loudon's pattern books and the writings of Lewis Cottingham and George Truefitt, Vaux's mentors in the domestic neo-Gothic style. Downing particularly regarded the Greek Revival style as too stark in juxtaposition with nature, which Vaux later agreed was "passionless." A revision of solid geometry in either house or town would permit the models to blend "with the outlines of American scenery," said Vaux.

The 25-year-old Vaux consequently came to Newburgh, N.Y., to help Downing establish a new residential style. With the changes occurring in American society, including the new interest in Transcendentalism, Vaux thought that the art of the American democracy should be an outdoors one. Such a political stance "demanded of art to thrive in the open in all weathers, for the benefit of all if it was worth anything, and if not, to perish as a troublesome and useless encumbrance," Vaux declared.

After Downing perished in 1852 during a steamboat race, Vaux operated the office until 1857 for his partner's widow, Caroline. He then moved to New York City and asked Frederick Law Olmsted to join him in the 1858 competition to design Central Park. Their proposal won over 33 entries, launching the movement to put "rural parks" in American cities.

Of all the urban reform movements of the mid-19th century, that of Paris was probably the most formal and imperial, that of New York City the most informal and democratic. This difference made possible parallel provisions for "rural recreation" in New York City and along the Hudson

Calvert Vaux, an Englishman who came to New York to work with Downing. (Society for the Preservation of New England Antiquities)

Vale of Cashmere, Prospect Park, Brooklyn, N.Y. Low and thick plantings added mystery to the pathway near the water. (Olmsted Associates)

Italianate Terrace, Central Park, New York City, 1858. This formal feature in a romantic park united and focused the more irregular elements. (*Third Annual Report of the Board of Commissioners of the Central Park*, 1860)

Rustic Arbor, Central Park. Benches around trees were a Vaux innovation. (Museum of the City of New York)

Mall, Central Park, with a cavernous arch of trees. (Olmsted and Kimball, *Forty Years of Landscape Architecture II: Central Park*)

River, something that could not take place in France. The means usually would be picturesque, rustic and amateurish, occasionally with formal touches because the age was so eclectic.

One such exception was Vaux's formal Italianate Terrace (1858) in Central Park, a therapeutic device inspired by the English genius of botany and structures, Joseph Paxton, and his "People's Park" (1857) in Halifax, in northeastern England, designed for workers of the huge carpet mills. Downing said of Paxton's earlier Italianate terrace (1825–50) at Chatsworth that it offered a vista "where you take in, without moving, all this magical landscape." Likewise, for New York City the inspiration came from handsome views of the Hudson Valley from estate terraces.

Leading back from Vaux's Italianate Terrace, and slightly more American and less English, was the Mall of Central Park, with trees arched over it. Downing had urged in *The Horticulturist* in 1847 that New Yorkers emulate the New England village street, with its tunnel of elms, chestnuts or maples. This same democratic, sheltering spread was created also for Central Park's Rustic Arbor. (Vaux liked this model from nature so much that it also appeared in the vaulted and skylighted interior that he and G. K. Radford proposed in their winning design for the unbuilt Main Pa-

Main Pavilion, Philadelphia Centennial Exhibition, a "forest" of nature and structure. (*New-York Sketchbook of Architecture*, 1874)

Aviary, Central Park, a contrast to the formal Italianate terrace. (*Central Park Reports*, 1862–64)

vilion of the 1876 Philadelphia Centennial Exhibition.)

For his most mature sylvan composition, Brooklyn's Prospect Park, Vaux furnished the first sketch in 1865 and then asked Olmsted to rejoin him from California to complete the project. This park reflected another of Paxton's precedents, Birkenhead Park (1843–47) near Liverpool. Its same curving self-containment was evident in Prospect Park, but with more differentiation among the three basic elements, "turf, wood, and water." Paxton rarely cultivated nostalgia or mystery, whereas Prospect Park exhibited them in the convolution and density of the midsection, known then as the Vale of Cashmere. Vaux continued his work on the park until 1870, Olmsted until 1873, the date of its completion.

Self-containment, advanced by sequential mystery, was also conveyed in Olmsted and Vaux's renowned suburb of Riverside, Ill. (1868–70), where, in effect, the city comes back into the park. Above the plan and under the trees, it attained a sheltering, spreading look similar to Central Park's Mall and Rustic Arbor and the interior of the Philadelphia Main Pavilion. Riverside was another stellar example of how landscape and architecture could be profitably blended in this new country. ✍

FREDERICK LAW OLMSTED
Charles E. Beveridge

Frederick Law Olmsted (1822–1903), the leading landscape architect of the post–Civil War generation and acknowledged father of American landscape architecture, created a firm that dominated the profession until World War II. With his first partner, Calvert Vaux, he designed Central Park (1858–63; 1865–78) and planned some 50 additional projects including Prospect Park (1865–73) in Brooklyn, Buffalo's northside park system (1868–76), Chicago's South Parks (1871) and the residential community of Riverside, Ill. (1868–70). Between 1872 and his retirement in 1895, he and his partners and staff carried out an additional 550 commissions, including Mount Royal Park (1874–81) in Montreal and Belle Isle Park (1881–84) in Detroit; the United States Capitol grounds (1874–91); the campuses of Lawrenceville School (1883–87) in New Jersey and Stanford University (1886–91); several park systems on which work continued beyond Olmsted's retirement, among them Buffalo's southside park system (1888) and systems in Boston (1878), Rochester, N.Y. (1888), and Louisville (1891); and his last two great projects, the site plan for the World's Columbian Exposition (1888–93) in Chicago and George W. Vanderbilt's Biltmore estate (1888–95) in Asheville, N.C.

Two of his most talented young students and partners, Henry Sargent Codman and Charles Eliot, died before him; but his stepson and partner, John Charles Olmsted, and his son and namesake, Frederick Law Olmsted, Jr., carried on his design tradition. As senior partners in the firm, they oversaw some 3,000 new projects between 1895 and 1950.

Born in Hartford, Conn., Olmsted moved to the New York City area in 1848 and finally settled in Brookline, Mass., in the early 1880s. The Olmsted firm remained in Brookline until 1980, when the National Park Service purchased his home and office to create the Olmsted National Historic Site. Olmsted drew his professional training from a variety of experiences. Between 1837, when illness prevented him from entering college, and his appointment as superintendent of Central Park in 1857, he was variously a clerk, seaman in the China trade, farmer, traveling correspondent in the slave-holding South for New York City newspapers and partner in a publishing firm. During the next eight years he was an administrator—first as architect-in-chief of Central Park, in charge of its construction; next as the administrative head of the U.S. Sanitary Commission (a Civil War forerunner of the American Red Cross); and then as manager of the vast Mariposa gold mining estate in California.

In all his activities Olmsted attempted to improve American society. He envisioned the creation of public institutions of culture and recreation, including parks, that would be available to all people. He also sought to foster "communitiveness"—a sense of shared community and dedicated service. His concept of the role of the landscape architect was as broad as his social and political concerns. The profession would shape the American city by designing public parks and park systems to meet a wide range of recreational needs. It would also create a new kind of community that was carefully planned for the single purpose of domestic life. Linked by rapid transit to a central-city working place, the residential suburb would make avail-

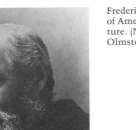

Frederick Law Olmsted, the father of American landscape architecture. (National Park Service, Olmsted NHS)

Plan for Prospect Park, Brooklyn, N.Y., a classic park design, demonstrating the flow of walks and drives leading the visitor through a series of landscapes. (National Park Service, Olmsted NHS)

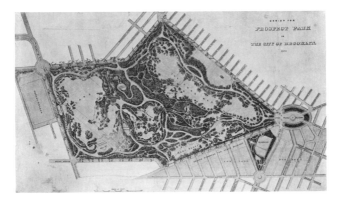

Long Meadow, Prospect Park, an expanse of pastoral scenery and an example of the "beautiful." (National Park Service, Olmsted NHS)

PROPOSED PLAN.

PRESENT PLAN.

Opposite top: Picturesque scenery of the Ramble, Central Park. (Herbert Mitchell)

Opposite center: Central Park's second transverse road for crosstown traffic. West Side Manhattan is in the background beyond Eighth Avenue. (The New-York Historical Society)

able the best aspects of city and country life. There, landscape architects would design residential grounds with numerous "open air apartments" by which domestic activities could be moved out of doors.

Olmsted had high expectations for the visual and psychological effects of his designs. He believed that "pastoral" park scenery, with a gracefully undulating greensward and scattered groves of trees, was a powerful antidote to the stress and artificiality of urban life. Such scenery, he suggested, unconsciously promoted a sense of tranquillity by subordinating individual elements in the landscape to the overall design. He heightened this sense of calm by carefully separating different landscape themes and conflicting uses. Olmsted applied these principles of separation and subordination more consistently than any other landscape designer of his era. Subordination is found in his parks, where carefully constructed walks and drives flow through the landscape with gentle grades and easy curves, requiring a viewer's minimal attention to the process of movement. At the same time, structures merge into the landscape. Separation is found in his park systems, where large parks designed for the enjoyment of scenery are supplemented by smaller recreational areas for other activities and where "park ways" handle the movement of pedestrian and vehicular traffic.

In addition to designing for urban living, Olmsted was anxious to preserve areas of great natural beauty for public enjoyment. He served as head of the first commission in charge of Yosemite Valley and was a leader in establishing the Niagara Reservation, which he planned with Calvert Vaux in 1887.

As a designer, Olmsted drew from American natural scenery, the social values of his native region and the writings of Andrew Jackson Downing and other precursors. At the same time he benefited from visiting the parks and landscapes of Britain and the Continent. He learned about landscape art from John Ruskin's writings and carefully studied the treatises on landscape and gardening by William Gilpin, Humphry Repton, Uvedale Price and William Robinson. Although he drew heavily from English traditions, he recognized the importance of developing distinctive landscape styles for the American South and Midwest, and while in California and Colorado he began to develop a water-conserving style appropriate to the semiarid American West.

As an American, Olmsted provided his fellow citizens with recreational and residential amenities that had previously been monopolized by the privileged classes of Europe. In addition, he sought to produce a landscape design profession that rejected mere decoration in order to create spaces meeting the social and psychological needs of Americans in a comprehensive and imaginative way. 🖋

Opposite: Section of Eastern Parkway, Brooklyn, 1868, showing Olmsted's concern with separate ways for different modes of traffic. (Library of Congress)

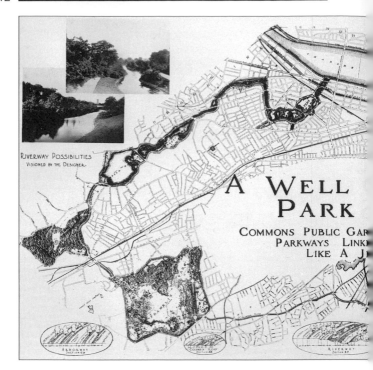

RIVERWAY POSSIBILITIES
VISIONED BY THE DESIGNER.

A WELL
PARK

COMMONS PUBLIC GAR
PARKWAYS LINK
LIKE A J

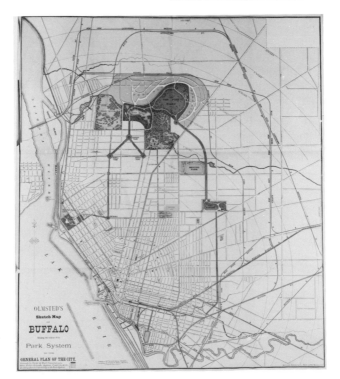

OLMSTED'S
Sketch Map
BUFFALO
Park System
GENERAL PLAN OF THE CITY.

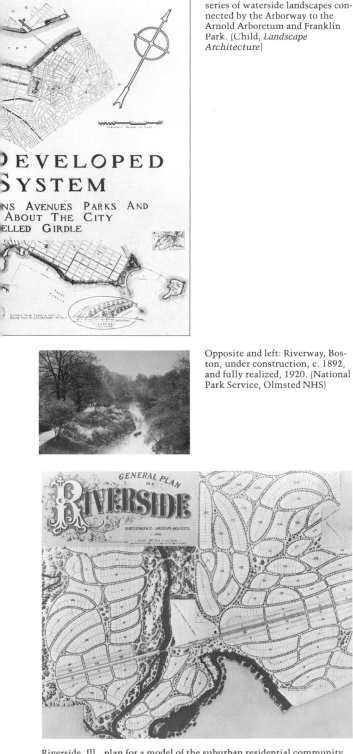

Boston's Emerald Necklace, a series of waterside landscapes connected by the Arborway to the Arnold Arboretum and Franklin Park. (Child, *Landscape Architecture*)

Opposite and left: Riverway, Boston, under construction, c. 1892, and fully realized, 1920. (National Park Service, Olmsted NHS)

Riverside, Ill., plan for a model of the suburban residential community. Curving streets create a sense of enclosure and discourage commercial through traffic. (National Park Service, Olmsted NHS)

Opposite: Buffalo's park system, c. 1876, a park and smaller recreational grounds linked by a series of parkways. (National Park Service, Olmsted NHS)

Congress Park, Saratoga Springs, N.Y., 1922. (George S. Bolster collection; H. B. Settle)

Jacob Weidenmann. (Miriam and Ira D. Wallach Division of Art, Prints and Photographs, New York Public Library)

JACOB WEIDENMANN
David Schuyler

Born in Winterthur, Switzerland, Jacob Weidenmann (1829–93) received professional training in Europe and worked as an architect and engineer before emigrating to the United States in 1856. Recognizing opportunities for landscape gardening in the New World, he studied the writings of Andrew Jackson Downing and John Claudius Loudon and, in 1859, moved to Hartford, Conn. There, he designed Bushnell Park, Cedar Hill Cemetery and several private residences while supervising the execution of Olmsted and Vaux's plan for the Hartford Retreat for the Insane.

The best indication of Weidenmann's early career can be found in his *Beautifying Country Homes* (1870), which contains seven of his landscape designs and advice to homeowners on how to "improve and beautify . . . suburban home(s)." Weidenmann's technical training is evident in the book's discussion of site engineering and planting design, and his principles of taste are apparent in the 24 handsome plates that embellish the text. Olmsted later described it as "a standard book," while critic Marianna Griswold Van Rensselaer included it in a list of the best works on landscape architecture published since 1820.

Near the time of the book's publication, Weidenmann journeyed to Europe to study "various public works of our profession." Returning in 1871, he moved to New York City, resuming his association with Olmsted and Vaux to work on Prospect Park in Brooklyn and superintend construction of several suburban estates. He became Olmsted's partner in 1874, and the two men designed Congress Park in Saratoga Springs, N.Y., and the Schuylkill Ar-

Pencil sketch of the music pavilion in Congress Park. (Miriam and Ira D. Wallach Division of Art, Prints and Photographs, New York Public Library)

Plan of Bushnell Park, Hartford, c.1859. (*Beautifying Country Homes*; John C. Freeman)

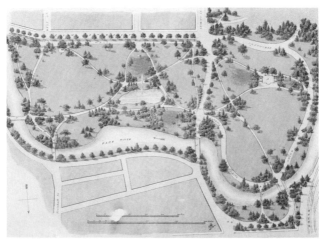

Cover of the first issue of *American Garden Architecture*, January 1877.
(Miriam and Ira D. Wallach Division of Art, Prints and Photographs,
New York Public Library)

Opposite: Watercolor of grounds near a road at Masquetux, Babylon,
N.Y. (Miriam and Ira D. Wallach Division of Arts, Prints and Photographs, New York Public Library)

senal outside Philadelphia. Weidenmann also helped
Olmsted prepare plans for Mount Royal Park in Montreal,
the United States Capitol grounds and other important
projects. In this work, Olmsted reported, "I found him well
informed, capable and efficient; and his duties were per-
formed to my satisfaction and that of all parties interested." While associated with Olmsted, Weidenmann prepared *American Garden Architecture* (1877–78), intending
it to be issued in 12 monthly installments. It was never
completed, but surviving segments include Weidenmann's
designs for kiosks, pavilions, bridges, cottages, green-
houses and gatehouses, along with explanatory notes.

At this time Weidenmann also worked independently on
suburban community plans for Hill Park Estate on Staten
Island, N.Y., and for Short Hills, N.J. He also designed a
number of private estates, including Henry B. Hyde's Masquetux in Babylon, N.Y., for which Weidenmann received
a medal and diploma from the United States Centennial
Commission in 1876.

As Weidenmann's reputation grew, he began receiving
commissions in the Midwest, including the Iowa State
Capitol grounds and a suburban subdivision in Des
Moines. Prospects for additional work induced him to accept the superintendence of Chicago's Mount Hope Ceme-

Plan of Hill Park Estate, near New Dorp, Staten Island, N.Y. (Staten Island Institute of Arts and Sciences)

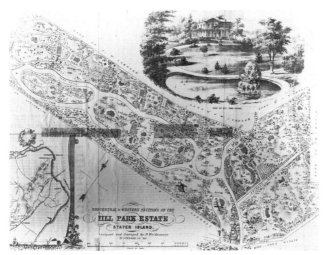

tery in 1886. Unfortunately, the cemetery proved to be a "mean land speculation," and Weidenmann was soon out of work. He did, however, assist architect William Le Baron Jenney on a number of projects and wrote the text of *Modern Cemeteries* (1888), which codified the principles of landscaping burial grounds. Olmsted asserted that Weidenmann was the "highest authority on the subject" and decidedly his superior "in this department of our profession."

After returning to New York City in 1889, Weidenmann's important later projects included designs for the Brooklyn College campus and Pope Park in Hartford, Conn. He died before completing the latter. The man who once remarked, "My destiny is to work for the grave diggers," was buried in Cedar Hill Cemetery, one of his first important projects.

Weidenmann brought thorough training to his chosen career, which he considered "this noblest of all Art professions." He urged the establishment of a professional school to raise landscape architecture "to proper standing in science and art." Appropriately, Harvard University awards a prize in his name to an outstanding student in landscape architecture, a fitting recognition of Weidenmann's accomplishments and his commitment to his profession. 🖋

JOHN CHARLES OLMSTED
Arleyn A. Levee

As senior partner of Olmsted Brothers from 1898 until his
death, John Charles Olmsted (1852–1920) presided over a
practice that grew from approximately 600 to more than
3,500 commissions. In a profession still without its first
training program or professional organization, Olmsted had
already been in active practice for 23 years as an associate
and junior partner of his stepfather and uncle, Frederick
Law Olmsted. On the retirement of the elder Olmsted and
the death of his partner, Charles Eliot, John Olmsted
formed Olmsted Brothers in 1898 with his younger step-
brother, Frederick Law Olmsted, Jr., then only four years
out of college. Shortly thereafter, the brothers became
founding members of the American Society of Landscape
Architects, with John Olmsted becoming its first president.
As such, he was largely responsible for establishing membership standards and codes of practice for the profession.

Frederick Law Olmsted had married his brother's widow
and adopted her children, including John, in 1859. During
John's formative years the family lived in Central Park,
then under construction, and in 1863–65 amid the splendors of the Sierra Nevada, where the elder Olmsted managed a gold-mining company. This western experience was
influential in teaching John to read natural land forms and
to identify plant materials. He reinforced this expertise
during the summers of 1869 and 1871, working with the
40th Parallel survey teams in the wilds of Nevada and
Utah. After being graduated from Yale University's Shef-
field Scientific School in 1875, he worked in his stepfather's office, becoming a full partner in 1884 when the
firm moved from New York City to Brookline, Mass. His
skills in art, architecture, engineering and photography enhanced the practice, while his management expertise
turned the office into an efficient business with a growing
staff.

Olmsted continued his stepfather's principles of design
in his diversified nationwide work. As communities became more densely populated and heterogenous, his emphasis changed from the pastoral to the more architectural
and recreational. He urged controls over haphazard building to protect important vistas and areas of outstanding
scenic beauty. His projects included comprehensive park
systems for Dayton, Seattle and Spokane, as well as Essex
County, N.J., Portland, Ore., Portland, Maine, and Fall
River, Mass. He expanded his stepfather's park and parkway designs in the Boston area, Louisville, Hartford,
Conn., Atlanta and Buffalo, Rochester and Brooklyn, N.Y.
He designed parks in numerous other cities, including
Charleston, S.C., and New Orleans. His work on the playgrounds of Chicago's South Parks introduced an innovative
approach to recreational planning as an extension of the
settlement house concept.

Institutional commissions included numerous schools
and universities, among them Smith, Mount Holyoke,
Amherst, Chicago, Washington, Iowa State and Ohio State,
as well as asylums, libraries, hospitals and state capitols.
Work with the elder Olmsted on the World's Columbian
Exposition of 1893 in Chicago led to commissions for expo-
sition grounds in Portland, Ore., Seattle and Winnipeg,
Manitoba. In Dayton, Olmsted's proposals for the National
Cash Register factory environs grew until he had shaped

John Charles Olmsted, 1907. (National Park Service, Olmsted NHS)

Plan of Orange Park, Essex County, N.J., 1900. (National Park Service, Olmsted NHS)

Pond in Orange Park, c. 1914, surrounded by rich plant growth. The carriage drive and path systems meandering through this oddly shaped park unify the passages through greensward and woodland and by water. (National Park Service, Olmsted NHS)

much of the city with his plans for the Oakwood and Hills and Dales subdivisions and the city's park system.

Although Olmsted's contributions to the development of the landscape architectural profession were great, his legacy in influencing the patterns of cities and their quality of life has been even greater. In the Olmsted firm's remarkable history, John Olmsted maintained the continuity of the practice while expanding its professional growth. As a link between 19th-century romanticism and 20th-century pragmatism, he provided an interpretation of Frederick Law Olmsted's vision in the vocabulary of a new era. 🐿

Below and right below: Park Number Two (Mark White Square), South Parks, Chicago. Now called McGuane Park, this space has been significantly altered in recent years. The original plan of 1904 provided a small urban park with a pool and beach enclosed in a tree-lined setting. (National Park Service, Olmsted NHS)

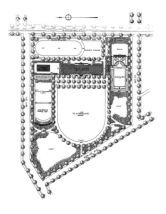

Plan for Mt. Holyoke College, South Hadley, Mass., 1900, soon revised to meet growing college needs. (National Park Service, Olmsted NHS)

Central Park, Louisville, c. 1908. Curving paths soften the geometry of this square urban park. (National Park Service, Olmsted NHS)

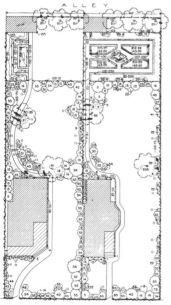

One of a series of residential designs proposed by Olmsted Brothers for employees of National Cash Register, Dayton, 1900. (National Park Service, Olmsted NHS)

Charles Eliot, 1896. (Penn State University)

Newburyport Commons, Newburyport, Mass. (E. Lynn Miller)

White Park, Concord, N.H., one of Eliot's early works. (E. Lynn Miller)

CHARLES ELIOT
E. Lynn Miller

Summer scientific expeditions to Mt. Desert Island off the coast of Maine sparked Charles Eliot's early interest in environmental management. Later, Eliot would become known for his natural-systems approach to landscape architecture.

Eliot (1859–97) was born in Cambridge, Mass., where his father was president of Harvard University. On graduation from Harvard in 1882, he pursued special horticultural courses at Bussey Institute to prepare himself for the profession of landscape architecture. In 1883 he became an apprentice for Frederick Law Olmsted and Company, where he worked on designs for Franklin Park (1884), the Arnold Arboretum (1885) and the Fens (1883) in Boston and Belle Isle Park (1884) in Detroit. On Olmsted's advice, Eliot traveled to Europe in 1885 to observe natural scenery as well as the landscape designs of Capability Brown, Humphry Repton, Joseph Paxton and Prince Pückler-Muskau. Eliot's travel diaries provide one of the best visual assessments of European landscapes in the late 19th century.

Returning to Boston in 1886, Eliot opened his own office and was immediately involved with work of considerable importance not only in the Boston area but also throughout the East. Noteworthy are White Park (1888) in Concord, N.H., Youngstown Gorge (1891), now called Mill Creek Park, in Youngstown, Ohio, and the plan (1890) for a new town in Salt Lake City.

In addition to his practice, Eliot became a regular contributor of professional articles to *Garden and Forest Magazine.* In February 1890 he wrote a landmark article entitled "Waverly Oaks" to defend a stand of virgin trees in Belmont, Mass. He made a plea for preservation of the oaks and outlined a strategy for conserving other areas of scenic beauty in the same way that the Boston Public Library held books and the Museum of Fine Arts pictures. The Waverly Oaks article resulted in an 1890 conference held at the Massachusetts Institute of Technology on preservation of scenic beauty and the enactment of state legislation creating the Trustees of Public Reservations in 1891—the first organization in the world established to "acquire, hold, protect and administer, for the benefit of the public, beautiful and historical places." Within two years, Eliot's concept was used to establish Britain's National Trust. Eliot's work with the Trustees of Public Reservations led to legislation in 1893 creating the Boston Metropolitan Park System, one of the first such systems in the world.

Following the untimely death of their partner Henry Sargent Codman, Frederick Law Olmsted and John Charles Olmsted pleaded with Eliot to join their firm. In March 1893 Eliot agreed, and the name was changed to Olmsted, Olmsted and Eliot. Within a few months, because of the elder Olmsted's failing health, Eliot assumed the leadership

Charles River, a tidal estuary and one of the key elements in Eliot's plan for Boston's Metropolitan Park System. (E. Lynn Miller)

role in the partnership. The firm was appointed landscape architect for the Boston Metropolitan Park Commission. In 1896 Eliot prepared a study, *Vegetation and Forest Scenery for the Reservation*, setting forth his concept of "landscape forestry" for rehabilitating the reservations to be included in the metropolitan park system. In preparing this seminal work, Eliot developed a methodology that moved the profession of landscape architecture from the era of intuitive design to a scientific, natural-systems approach.

Eliot died in 1897 at the threshold of a brilliant career. His death was an irreparable loss to the field of landscape architecture and the American environmental movement. Although eulogies proclaimed Eliot as the father of the Boston Metropolitan Park System, the most fitting memorial to his greatness as a landscape architect came in 1900 when the first university course of professional training in landscape architecture was established at Harvard. 🖋

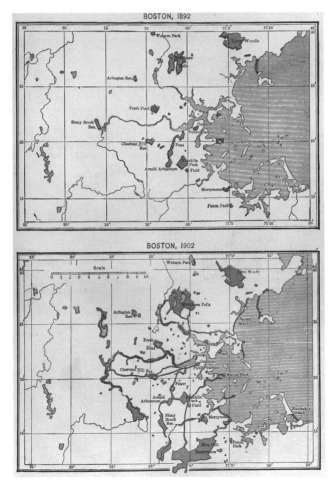

Open spaces surrounding the Boston area in 1892 compared to 1902. The amount of land devoted to open space increased because of Eliot's work with the Trustees of Public Reservations. (Eliot, *Charles Eliot, Landscape Architect*)

WARREN H. MANNING
William Grundmann

Warren H. Manning (1860–1938) began his career working in his father's nursery in Reading, Mass. From 1888 to 1896 he was employed by Frederick Law Olmsted and John Charles Olmsted in their Brookline office. With his extensive knowledge of plant materials, he was placed in charge of most of the office's planting plans, completing 125 projects in 22 states, including the designs for the World's Columbian Exposition of 1893 and Biltmore (1888–95) in Asheville, N.C.

In 1896 Manning became an independent landscape designer, completing projects he had initiated in the Olmsted office and securing work from the many clients he had met there. He formed a partnership with his brother J. Woodward Manning in 1901, calling the firm Manning Brothers. Four years later the partnership dissolved, and Warren continued practicing under his own name in Cambridge, Mass.

The Manning office did a wide range of work from 1896 until his death, including numerous estate plans for influential and rich clients such as Rockefeller, McCormick, Griscom, Peavy, Sprague and Seiberling. City plans were completed for Athens, Ga., Birmingham, Ala., Harrisburg, Pa., and Warren, Ariz. City, state and national parks also were part of Manning's legacy. These included parks and park systems for Milwaukee, Minneapolis, St. Paul, Louisville, Cincinnati, and Harrisburg, Wilkes-Barre, Steelton and Kistler, Pa. Plans for state parks were created for Watkins Glen and Bluff Point reservations in New York and for national parks including Yellowstone's Hot Spring Reservation and Gardiner Gate. Campus plans and design recommendations were prepared for state universities throughout the country. Elementary and high school plans also were completed for locations in 15 states.

In the second decade of the 20th century, Manning began organizing and developing a "National Plan for America." During his many trips throughout the country for the Olmsted office and later on his own, he perceived a need to focus national development to take better advantage of nat-

Dolobran, estate of C. A. Griscom, Philadelphia, 1900. (Iowa State University)

Warren H. Manning, 1938. (*Landscape Architecture Quarterly*)

Ponds and stream running through the estate of Thomas Lowry, Monticello, Minn., 1902. (Iowa State University)

Formal garden on the estate of G. W. Mather, Cleveland, 1909, with typical elements of Manning's estate design, including potted plants and a gravel walkway. (Iowa State University)

Garden on the estate of Finley Barrell, Lake Forest, Ill., 1912. (Iowa State University)

ural conditions. He maintained that towns, cities, manufacturing complexes and other economic units should be close to natural resources and transportation corridors. He further believed that state boundaries should be located according to geological formations and not as arbitrary lines drawn on a map. Manning's study resulted in a "National Plan Study Brief" published in *Landscape Architecture* (1923). Unfortunately, the full 900-page report was never published.

Manning's work followed in the tradition of the Olmsted office, while he continued to perfect and establish an approach to planting design emulating the natural landscape but also integrating formal plantings and structured gardens. He was a charter member of the American Society of Landscape Architects and was a driving force in founding the organization in 1899. His early park designs became the foundation for open space systems now found in many major American cities. With thoughtful restoration they can provide a legacy that will last for many years. 🖉

Study for landscape setting, Cleveland Museum of Art, 1909. (Iowa State University)

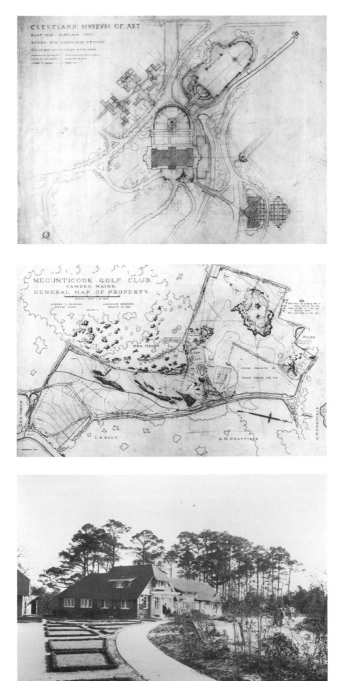

Above: Exposition in Jamestown, Va., 1910. (Iowa State University)

Center: Plan of Megunticook Golf Club, Camden, Maine, 1913. (Iowa State University)

FREDERICK LAW OLMSTED, JR.
Shary Page Berg

By his very name, Frederick Law Olmsted, Jr. (1870–1957), was destined to become a landscape architect and a leader in guiding the growth and philosophy of the profession established by his father. Together their careers spanned 100 years. He was a founding member, and later president, of the American Society of Landscape Architects; he established the first formal training program in landscape architecture, at Harvard University, in 1900; and his prolific writings and extensive service on various boards and commissions made him a highly visible figure.

The younger Olmsted began his career as an apprentice on the World's Columbian Exposition of 1893. His second major assignment was as his father's on-site representative at Biltmore (1888–95) in North Carolina. Following the elder Olmsted's retirement, the firm became Olmsted Brothers in 1898, with John Charles Olmsted and Frederick Law Olmsted, Jr., as equal partners. John Olmsted, 18 years older and far more experienced, was an excellent administrator and skilled designer. The young Olmsted was more of a public figure. After John Olmsted's death in 1920, Frederick Law Olmsted, Jr., was senior partner until his retirement in 1950.

In 1901 Olmsted began a 50-year involvement with the nation's capital when he was appointed to the Senate Park Commission, charged with updating the plan of Washington, D.C., and guiding the city's growth into the 20th century. The McMillan Plan, as it came to be known, is largely responsible for establishing the outline of the present city. Olmsted is credited with the emphasis on a system of regional parks extending into the surrounding suburbs.

The early 20th century was a time of growing civic pride and emerging awareness of the need for orderly community growth. As a leader in the new city planning movement,

Cross sections of typical streets from a city plan for Newport, R.I., 1913. Large trees in the drawings depict existing trees. (National Park Service, Olmsted NHS)

Frederick Law Olmsted, Jr. (National Park Service, Olmsted NHS)

Drafting room at the Olmsted office, 1930. (National Park Service, Olmsted NHS)

Plan for the Mall, Washington, D.C., 1901, a portion of the McMillan Plan. The United States Capitol is on the far right. (National Capital Planning Commission)

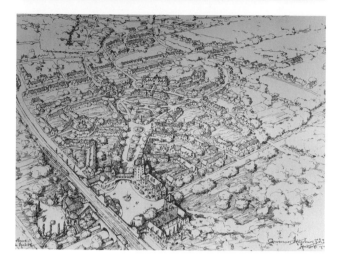

Olmsted prepared studies for several communities including Boulder, Colo. (1910), New Haven, Conn. (1910), Rochester, N.Y. (1911), Newport, R.I. (1913), and Pittsburgh (1923). He also designed private residential communities including Forest Hills Gardens (1911) in Queens, N.Y., portions of Roland Park (1920s) in Baltimore, where work by the Olmsted firm had begun in the 1890s, and Palos Verdes Estates (1923) near Los Angeles. While much of his career embraced planning, he was also a skilled designer whose projects included residences, estates and parks.

Olmsted's interest in conservation began early and continued throughout his life. His first major contribution shaped the 1916 legislative mandate of the National Park Service. He also worked on projects for the national parks from Acadia to the Everglades to the Olympics, but his most active role was at Yosemite, where he was on the board of advisers for many years. A leader in the state and regional park movement, he was landscape architect (1898–1920) for the Boston Metropolitan Park System after the death of Charles Eliot and formulated the plan (1929) that resulted in California's extensive state park system.

Both Olmsteds, senior and junior, were at the forefront of their profession. Any differences in their approaches can be attributed to the era in which each worked. Under the guidance of the senior Olmsted, the field became known as landscape architecture, while Frederick Law Olmsted, Jr., began his career when the profession was well established. He sought, therefore, to refine and institutionalize it through his own work as well as through teaching and involvement in the American Society of Landscape Architects. And where the elder Olmsted was concerned with how landscape could provide recreational and health benefits for the entire population, the son was devoted to order and the public good in a more abstract sense, working on comprehensive planning, often on a regional scale.

The younger Olmsted's greatest strength was his ability to organize and systematize, whether developing guidelines for professional practice, criteria for selecting state parks or his own firm's filing system. His work spanned six decades during a time of unprecedented change, and his tremendous output, from detailed design and engineering schemes to broad planning and policy reports, reflects the growth and dynamism of the field. ✍

Opposite: Aerial sketch of Forest
Hills Gardens, Queens, N.Y.,
1910. (National Park Service,
Olmsted NHS)

Plan for the Olmsted residence,
Palos Verdes Estates, Calif., 1927.
(National Park Service, Olmsted
NHS)

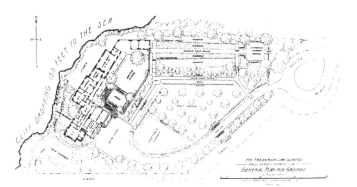

Center and above: Palos Verdes Estates, a 16,000-acre planned residential
community, shown here early in its development. (National Park Service, Olmsted NHS)

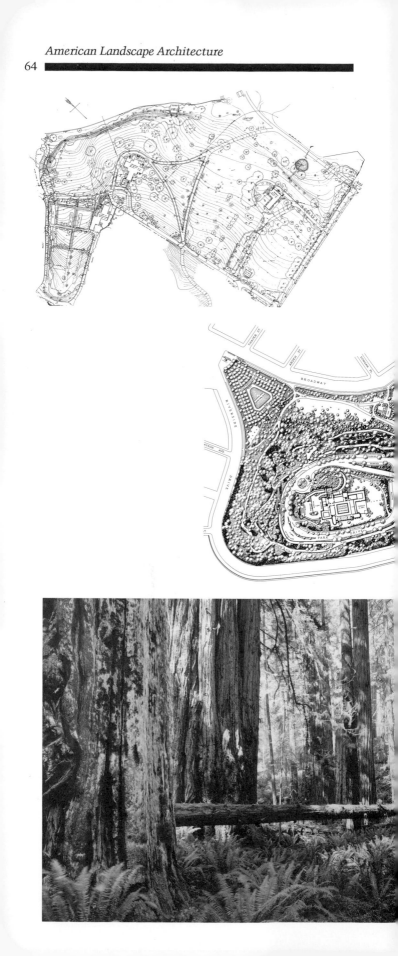

Opposite: Henry de Forest estate, Oyster Bay, N.Y., with both naturalistic landscaping and a more formal garden. (National Park Service, Olmsted NHS)

Plan for Fort Tryon Park, New York City, 1935, showing the complex circulation and extensive engineering required to create a park on this site. (National Park Service, Olmsted NHS)

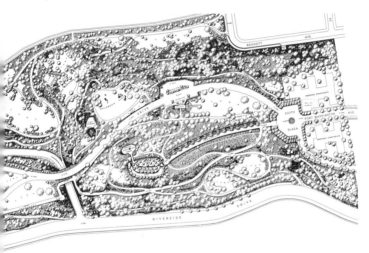

Frederick Law Olmsted Grove, Prairie Creek Redwoods State Park, northern California, dedicated to Olmsted for his strong advocacy of natural resource conservation. (National Park Service, Olmsted NHS)

Henry Vincent Hubbard, 1948.
(Frizell Studio; *Landscape
Architecture*)

Plan for Moss Hill, Boston, 1916,
one of the projects included in
Hubbard and Kimball's textbook,
*An Introduction to the Study of
Landscape Design*. Elbert Peets
executed the drawing as a member
of Hubbard's firm, Pray, Hubbard
and White.

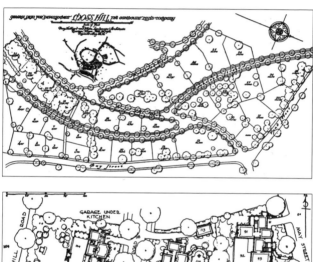

Plan and sectional drawings for several lots at Moss Hill, also from *Landscape Design*.

HENRY VINCENT HUBBARD
Kenneth I. Helphand

Henry Vincent Hubbard's reputation rests on his achievements as an educator and author. Born in Taunton, Mass., Hubbard (1875–1947) was educated at Harvard University. Subsequently, he completed the Massachusetts Institute of Technology's course in architecture, undertook independent studies in landscape architecture with Frederick Law Olmsted, Jr., and went on to receive Harvard's Lawrence Scientific School's first degree in landscape architecture in 1901. Professionally, he served a five-year apprenticeship with Olmsted Brothers (1901–06), practiced in Boston with Pray, Hubbard and White (1906–18), worked on wartime housing projects during World War I, including one in Hilton, Va., and in 1920 returned to Olmsted Brothers as a partner.

At Harvard from 1906 until 1941, Hubbard pioneered the development of the profession as a professor of landscape architecture and as the first chairman of both the School of City Planning (1929) and later the Department of Regional Planning. He also was a design and planning consultant to the Federal Housing Administration, Tennessee Valley Authority, National Park Service and the cities of Boston, Baltimore and Providence. Hubbard served as a member of the National Capital Park and Planning Commission and as president of the American Society of Landscape Architects (1931–34).

With John Nolen, Hubbard wrote two seminal planning studies, *Airports* (1930) and *Parkways and Land Values* (1937). "I believed, and still believe, that regional planning is based first on a recognition of the topography, the economics, the law, the political machinery, the predispositions, and backgrounds of the people who are to be served, or more properly, who are to be enabled to serve themselves," he wrote. He hoped for regional planning to emerge in America, "not as the adopted child of any other profession, but an essential common effort calling upon all those who can think creatively."

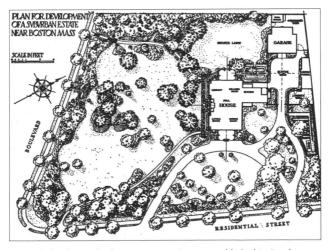

General plan for a suburban estate near Boston, published in *Landscape Design*.

Plan from *Landscape Design* showing the relationship of a house to views on all four sides.

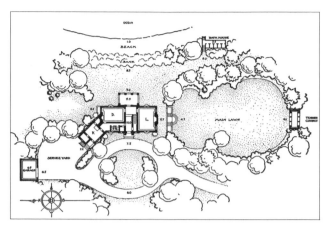

View over the meadow, The Park, Muskau, Germany. (Henry V. Hubbard)

In 1910 Hubbard founded, with C. D. Lay and Robert Wheelwright, the American Society of Landscape Architects' official journal, *Landscape Architecture*. Hubbard remained editor until his death 37 years later, writing numerous articles, editorials and reviews on topics as diverse as Italian garden theaters, land subdivision, recreational standards and the role of landscape architects in the National Park Service.

In 1917 he published with Theodora Kimball, Harvard's pioneering librarian in landscape architecture and city planning, *An Introduction to the Study of Landscape Design*. Revised in 1929, it was the profession's standard text for decades. The collaboration between Hubbard and Kimball blossomed into marriage in 1924. Together they also founded and served as editors of the journal *City Planning* and wrote *Our Cities To-day and To-morrow: A Survey of Planning and Zoning Progress in the United States* (1929). Their writings were a direct link to an Olmstedian philosophy tempered with 20th-century concerns. They were among pioneers such as Frederick Law Olmsted, Jr., James Sturgis Pray, John Nolen, Arthur Comey, Earle Draper, Hare and Hare and Henry Wright, all of whom built on landscape architecture's dual heritage as a fine art and a profession of social environmental reform to establish the planning profession in the United States. 🖋

Plan for the Wild Garden on a Newport, R.I., estate, 1916, from *Landscape Design*.

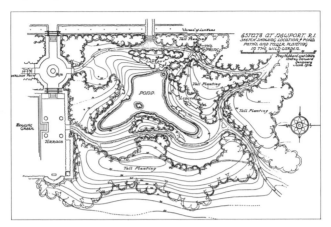

Spring in the Wild Garden. (Henry V. Hubbard)

Study for different types of steps in the Hubbard-Kimball textbook.

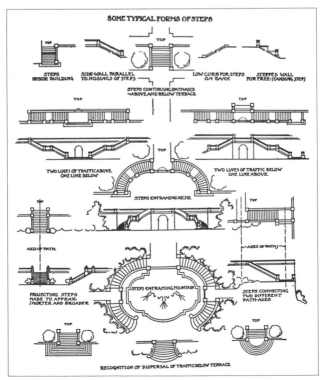

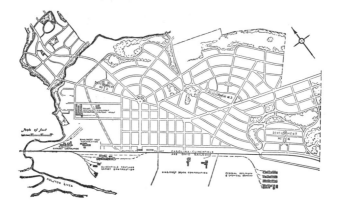

JOHN NOLEN
John L. Hancock

John Nolen (1869–1937) was a pioneering practitioner, author and educator in modern city and regional planning. The first American to identify himself exclusively as a town and city planner, he was at the forefront of the planning profession's evolution in the first two great eras of societal reform in the newly urbanized and industrialized United States: the Progressive movement (1900–17) and the New Deal (1930s).

Nolen's firm on Harvard Square in Cambridge, Mass., completed more than 400 commissions between 1904 and 1937. These included comprehensive plans for 50 new towns and suburbs, 51 cities and metropolitan areas and 18 regions and states; designs for park and parkway systems, subdivisions, civic and commercial centers, colleges and factories; and related studies. An informed, forceful speaker and writer, Nolen wrote seminal books and articles on planning and helped establish, and taught in, the nation's first planning degree programs at Harvard University and the Massachusetts Institute of Technology. Several associates including Phillip Foster, Justin Hartzog, Hale Walker and numerous other employees went on to establish distinguished careers.

One of a handful of Americans and Europeans in various fields who championed city planning as a vital element of reform, Nolen was an appropriate pioneer. From a lower middle-class Philadelphia family, he worked from early childhood, was graduated with honors from Girard College and the University of Pennsylvania, and administered a university adult education program for 10 years before studying landscape architecture at Harvard for a career in "civic improvement." Nolen shared with Charles Eliot, the Olmsteds and Patrick Geddes the design credo, "What is fair must be fit [and provide] fully for the plain necessities of living." Consistent with his training in landscape design, he was organically oriented and conservation

Opposite: Plan for Mariemont, Ohio, 1921, a new town east of Cincinnati that was called a "town for the motor age" by the *New York Times*. (Nolen, *New Towns for Old*)

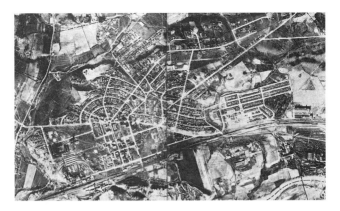

Opposite and above: Plan for
Kingsport, Tenn., 1916–21, and a
1936 aerial view. (*New Towns for
Old*; Piquet, *Kingsport,
Tennessee*)

John Nolen. (State Historical Society of Wisconsin)

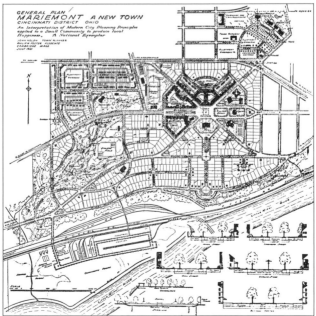

Plan for Walpole, Mass., 1913, linking three towns with parkways and riverside parks. (*New Towns for Old*)

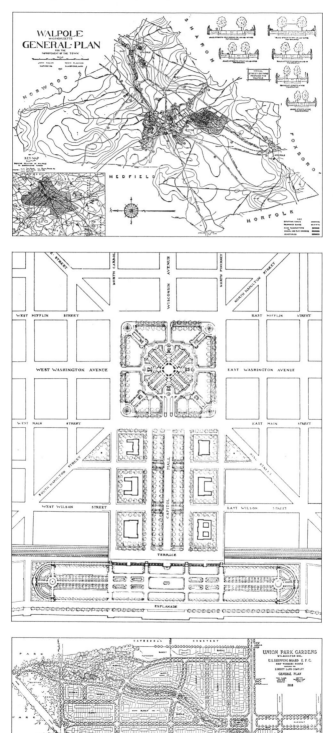

Above: Plan for Union Park Gardens, Wilmington, Del., 1918, a federal housing project. (*New Towns for Old*)

Center: Detail of Madison, Wis., plan linking the state capitol with the Lake Monona shoreline. (Nolen, *Madison: A Model City*)

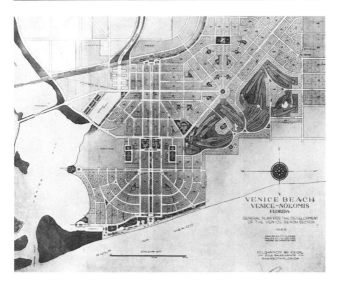

Plan for Venice, Fla., 1925, originally designed for the Brotherhood of Locomotive Engineers. (*New Towns for Old*)

minded in adapting the physical environment for human habitat.

Although Nolen was a pragmatic designer who believed that there was "no absolute rule [but only local opportunities arising] from different physical, historical and social conditions," his works portray several common characteristics: naturalistic open space; contoured streets and gateways; neighborhood elements (homes, streets, shops, parks, playgrounds) treated as basic units of the city system; natural and built barriers—the central design motif in his work—to separate functional areas and screen incompatible functions (industry, high-speed traffic, districts linked by parks, parkways, open spaces); major civic buildings grouped in a traditional, neoclassical way; decentralization of the city through merger with its suburbs; and emphasis on the welfare of the whole urban region and all of its residents.

Above all, his most important works are distinguished by a careful integration of physical, social, economic and political planning, as in the replanning of Madison, Wis. (1911), Walpole, Mass. (1911–35), and San Diego (1908, 1926); the new town plans for Kingsport, Tenn. (1915–21), Mariemont, Ohio (1923), and Venice, Fla. (1925); the tri-state Philadelphia regional plan (1931); and industrial housing subdivisions such as Union Park Gardens (1918) in Wilmington, Del.

Nolen's significance, and his great strength, lies in this holistic approach to planning and in his powers of persuasion in promoting and professionalizing city and regional planning. Instinctively democratic, egalitarian and kindly, he was a scholarly, articulate leader of planning thought and practice. "He saw the city as a whole, as a place for living, a work of art as well as a machine," said Russell Van-Nest Black, a former employee. A fellow of the American Society of Landscape Architects, president of the National Conference on City Planning and of the American City Planning Institute and the first American to head the International Federation of Housing and Town Planning, Nolen at the end of his career was considered the dean of American city planning. 🙠

OSSIAN COLE SIMONDS
Robert E. Grese

During the late 1800s, several landscape architects forged a uniquely midwestern style of landscape design. Among the leaders of this group was Ossian Cole Simonds (1857–1931) of Chicago. Known as O. C. to his friends and associates, Simonds created cemeteries, parks, residences and subdivisions throughout the Midwest, always trying to maintain the essential qualities of the native landscape.

Born in Grand Rapids, Mich., Simonds developed an early love for the fields and forests around his father's farm. Later, while a civil engineering student at the University of Michigan, he studied architecture under William Le Baron Jenney. After graduation in 1878, Simonds went to work for Jenney in his Chicago office. There, he laid out additions to Graceland Cemetery, a project that began in 1878 and would continue throughout his career, leading to work on other cemeteries around the country as well as to Simonds's reputation as dean of cemetery design.

Intending to practice architecture, Simonds became a member of the firm of Holabird, Simonds and Roche from 1880 to 1883. His work at Graceland Cemetery convinced him, however, that his true calling was that of a landscape gardener. In 1903 he established the firm of O. C. Simonds and Company, which became Simonds and West in 1925. As a landscape gardener, a name he preferred to landscape architect, Simonds developed a wide-ranging practice designing parks, campus plans, estates and subdivisions in addition to his cemetery work. While his activities were centered in the Midwest, at the time of his death the American Civic Association reported that he had worked in every state of the union.

An ardent supporter of the young profession of landscape architecture, Simonds was one of the founding members of the American Society of Landscape Architects. In 1913 he was the first noneasterner to be elected its president. He was also active in the American Civic Association and

Entrance, Graceland Cemetery, where Simonds worked off and on throughout his life. (University of Michigan)

served as chairman of its Rural Improvements Department. Moving in the same circle of friends as Jens Jensen and many of Chicago's Prairie School architects during the early 1900s, Simonds belonged to such groups as the Illinois Out-Door Improvement Association, the City Club, the Cliff Dwellers and the University Club. In 1908 he began teaching landscape design courses at the University of Michigan and was instrumental in establishing its landscape architecture program.

Simonds's design philosophy was perhaps best expressed in his book *Landscape Gardening* (1920). He emphasized the need for studying nature thoroughly as an inspiration for design. His projects featured carefully shaped topography with paths and roads placed to reveal a site's characteristic land forms. An ardent promoter of native plants, Simonds made extensive use of certain shrubs and trees then regarded as common weeds. He argued that the ultimate goal of landscape design should be to teach people to take pride in their surroundings and to see nature's subtle beauty around them.

During his lifetime, Simonds saw rampant destruction of the natural landscape as midwestern cities flourished. He used his design talents to reveal the regional landscape's inherent beauty and to inspire people "to respect the wooded bluffs and hillsides, the springs, streams, riverbanks, and lakeshores within the city boundaries and preserve them with tender loving care." Many of his writings and lectures were directed to the general public, emphasizing how they could take part in improving their surroundings. He recognized the importance of time in creating landscape designs and suggested that the landscape gardener should be "a dreamer, a designer, an inventor, a creator—a dreamer more than most designers because it takes years for his designs to develop."

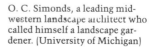

Path, Graceland Cemetery, a quiet sylvan setting created through the use of native trees and shrubs. (University of Michigan)

O. C. Simonds, a leading midwestern landscape architect who called himself a landscape gardener. (University of Michigan)

Below: Lake Hazelmere, Graceland Cemetery. (University of
Michigan)

Opposite: Hibbard residence,
Winnetka, Ill., c. 1914. (*Country
Life in America*, 1914)

Residential design for Julia Larned, Hubbard Woods, Ill. Such designs
usually included a network of outdoor rooms surrounded by shrubbery
and small trees. (University of Michigan)

Opposite: Pond at Locke Ledge,
Yorktown Heights, N.Y., estate of
Mrs. Arthur H. Marks, c. 1930.
(ASLA, *Illustrations of Work of
Members*, 1931)

Houghteling residence, Winnetka, Ill., c. 1912. Shrubs separate the house from the tennis court. (*Country Life in America*, 1912)

Sinnissippi Farm, Oregon, Ill., c. 1913, estate of Col. Frank O. Lowden. (*Country Life in America*, 1913)

JENS JENSEN
Stephen Christy

Jens Jensen (1860–1951), a colorful figure in American landscape architecture, was born in Dybbol, Denmark. He emigrated to America in 1884, settling in Chicago as a laborer for the West Chicago Park District and finding there the inspiration for his uniquely American art.

Few people have lived at a more propitious time for their profession. In his lifetime, Jensen witnessed the development of the suburbs predicted by Andrew Jackson Downing in the 1840s; Olmsted and Vaux's Central Park, the first of a generation of great urban landscape parks; the "back-to-nature" movement exemplified by Liberty Hyde Bailey's magazine, *Country Life in America*; the birth of the playground and recreation movements; and the appearance of the Prairie School, a loosely knit band of writers, artists, architects and landscape architects. The last two originated in Chicago, and Jensen was active in both.

Advancing rapidly within the city's park system, Jensen became the foreman of Union and Humboldt parks, then located in one of Chicago's most fashionable sections. After an abrupt political dismissal in 1900, he developed a lucrative private practice centered largely on the new estates springing up along Chicago's wealthy North Shore. Many of the city's most powerful citizens befriended him, and his reputation was secured.

In 1906 Jensen returned to the West Parks as general superintendent and chief landscape architect. He proceeded to reshape Garfield, Humboldt, Douglas and other smaller parks in his own style, collaborating with other Prairie School figures including architects Hugh Garden and John van Bergen. These parks, largely rebuilt by 1910, became the first full public expression of the prairie spirit in landscape architecture. This spirit, a regional manifestation of design tenets developed by Olmsted and other early landscape architects, was meant to impart to the viewer the essence of America's heartland.

Edward L. Ryerson estate (1912), Lake Forest, Ill., showing the meadow from the terrace. (Robert Fine; Jensen Collection, Morton Arboretum)

Top and above: Symbolic prairie expanse and an outdoor room, Ryerson estate. The property today preserves some of Jensen's finest vistas. (Robert Fine; Jensen Collection, Morton Arboretum)

Jens Jensen. (Jensen Collection, Morton Arboretum)

West Park Extension, Chicago.
The shaded areas indicate proposed additions. (Eaton, *Landscape Artist in America*, 1964)

Left and below: Fair Lane (1914–20), the estate of Henry Ford, Dearborn, Mich. This dam on the Rouge River is perhaps the best remaining example of Jensen's use of stratified limestone. (Robert Fine; Jensen Collection, Morton Arboretum)

Jensen's designs were both democratic and spiritual, expressing the fervent belief that America would develop a new culture rooted in its own regional landscapes. His symbols became the hawthorne, with its horizontal branches mimicking the prairie; low, gentle contours repeating the midwestern plains; and spectacular rockwork and waterfalls suggesting ravines and bluffs found along Lake Michigan and the Mississippi River. Columbus Park (1918), his last great public work in Chicago, incorporated these and other symbols to capture the soul of the midwestern landscape in an urban center.

During the 1920s, with the waning of the Prairie School and deepening political corruption in Chicago, Jensen's interests turned elsewhere—back to his childhood experiences in the "folk schools" of Denmark. His attendance at such a school in the 1870s had planted in him a lifelong belief in the purity of country life and art. Accordingly, in 1935 he founded the Clearing, his "school of the soil," located on spectacular bluffs overlooking Green Bay in the then-remote northern tip of Wisconsin's Door County. There, he spent his remaining years directing a unique institution that stressed the melding of physical labor and intellectual pursuits. The school continues to operate today along much the same lines.

Jensen stands out among American landscape architects for his view of landscape architecture as a social force in shaping a love of art, home life and landscape heritage. A man of great vision and powerful personality, he remained active and vigorous into his early 90s. At his death the *New York Times* gave him the well-earned title of dean of American landscape architects. 🖋

Council ring above Lake Springfield, Lincoln Memorial Garden
(1936), Springfield, Ill. Such rings served as settings for song, dance,
drama and readings. (Robert Fine; Jensen Collection, Morton
Arboretum)

Jensen at the Clearing, his "school of the soil," c. 1937. (Jensen Collection, Morton Arboretum)

Lake Michigan shoreline from the main lodge at the Clearing. (William H. Tishler)

Left and opposite center: Racine Parks, Racine, Wis. Jensen especially favored the contrast between a shady foreground and a sunny clearing beyond. (Robert Fine; Jensen Collection, Morton Arboretum)

CHARLES A. PLATT
Keith N. Morgan

Although Charles A. Platt (1861–1933) attracted national attention for his work as an etcher, painter and architect, he also made significant contributions to American landscape history in his gardens for country houses from the 1890s through the early 1930s.

Platt was born into a comfortable and cultured New York City family. Privately educated, he began his artistic education at the Art Students League and the National Academy of Design before going to Paris in 1880 to study landscape painting. Visits to Italy during his student years initiated his interest in landscape architecture. In 1894 he published *Italian Gardens*, the first illustrated book in English on Italian Renaissance gardens. Here, he introduced to American architecture and landscape architecture the ideal of the Italian villa, the concept of house and garden designed as a whole—organized as a series of indoor and outdoor rooms. Platt's interpretation of the villa in his book brought him some celebrity at home, along with commissions as a landscape architect despite his lack of formal training.

Platt began experimenting with garden design at Cornish, N.H., where he was a member of the summer art colony from 1889 until his death. His own garden, begun in 1892, suggests at a modest scale the principles that would underlay his subsequent landscape work: the total interrelationship of architecture and landscape using the axial connection of major rooms with geometrically arranged garden units. In gardens and houses for other members of the Cornish Colony, especially High Court (1891), his project for neighbor Annie Lazarus, he blended his vision of the Italian villas with regional materials of the New Hampshire hills.

A major step in his progression from amateur to professional was the commission he received in 1897 to design the grounds for Faulkner Farm, Charles Sprague's estate in Brookline, Mass. The project allowed Platt to explore his adaptations of Italian ideals on a grander scale. Platt used

Platt's residence (1892–1912), Cornish, N.H. (Richard Cheek)

Portrait of Charles A. Platt, by Thomas W. Dewing, 1893. (Private collecion; Richard Cheek)

Plan for Platt's residence showing the interrelationship of the house and the geometric garden units. (Platt office papers; Richard Cheek)

Plan for Faulkner Farm (1897–98), the estate of Charles Sprague,
Brookline, Mass. (Platt office papers; Richard Cheek)

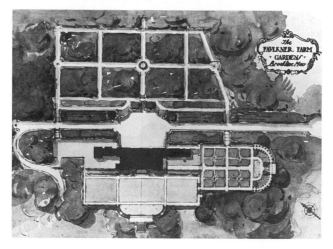

the characteristically Italian elements of a woodland garden, a broad grass terrace and a geometric flower garden to
embrace the Sprague mansion on three sides. Like many
other designers of his generation, he believed that modern
American architecture and landscapes should be derived
from a careful study of appropriate precedents.

Following the success of Faulkner Farm, Platt established an office as an architect and landscape architect. By
1904, when a major review of his work was published in
Architectural Record, he had become one of the leading designers of country houses and gardens. A monograph on his
work was published in 1913. Notable among his many influential commissions are three estates on the Great Lakes:
Gwinn (1907–08), the William Mather property near
Cleveland; the Moorings (1908–10), Russell Alger's estate
at Grosse Pointe, Mich.; and Villa Turicum (1908–18), the
Lake Forest, Ill., country place of Harold and Edith Rockefeller McCormick, the largest and most elaborate garden
of his career. For the McCormicks, Platt's landscape included polo grounds, walled kitchen gardens and expansive
pleasure grounds near the house featuring complex terraces, fountains and water staircases descending to the
shores of Lake Michigan.

Platt's country house landscapes were supplemented by
a small number of residential subdivisions and campus
plans. He frequently collaborated with other landscape architects, especially the Olmsted brothers on large-scale site
planning and Ellen Biddle Shipman on planting plans.
While he was not a member of professional landscape organizations, Platt exerted a dominant influence on the development of American residential landscape design through
his distinctive architectonic integration of house and
garden. 🖋

Garden pavilion and pergola, Faulkner Farm, an outgrowth of Platt's Italian travels. (Platt office papers; Richard Cheek)

Garden pavilion at Villa Lante, Bagnaia, Italy, photographed by Platt in 1892. Such settings evoked for the landscape architect an Italian ideal he attempted to replicate in his own designs. (Charles A. Platt)

Detail of the Weld garden, Larz Anderson estate, Brookline, Mass., 1901.
(Society for the Preservation of New England Antiquities)

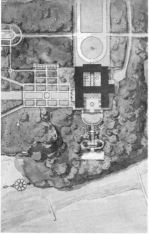

Plan for Villa Turicum (1908–18),
Lake Forest, Ill. (Platt office
papers; Richard Cheek)

Plan for the 1922–31 redevelopment of Phillips Academy, Andover, Mass. (Platt office papers; Richard Cheek)

Garden at Villa Turicum, the estate of Harold and Edith Rockefeller McCormick. (Platt office papers; Richard Cheek)

ELLEN BIDDLE SHIPMAN
Leslie Rose Close

Ellen Biddle Shipman (1870–1950) belonged to the generation of American women landscape architects active in the
early decades of this century. In an interview with the *New
York Times* in 1938, in fact, she attributed the renaissance
in garden design during these decades to the influence of
the increased number of women in the field.

Born to a wealthy Philadelphia family, Ellen McGowan
Biddle was educated at Radcliffe College. Her extensive
knowledge of plants and horticulture was essentially self-
taught, however, and while she was clearly gifted in this
realm, her family opposed her interest in a career in landscape architecture. It was Charles A. Platt who recognized
Shipman's talent for design, encouraging her to become a
landscape architect and giving her early opportunities for
work on several of his commissions. Platt was both mentor and collaborator for Shipman, and he had as profound
an influence on her work as he had on the profession of
landscape architecture. Platt's book *Italian Gardens* (1894)
espoused the collaboration between architecture and landscape architecture that would become emblematic of the
great gardens of the period. As a result of her training with
Platt, Shipman's work was extraordinarily facile architec-
turally, and she often designed complicated structures as
well as interiors.

Shipman taught for many years at the Lowthorpe School
of Landscape Architecture, Gardening and Horticulture for
Women, which, along with the Cambridge School of Architecture and Landscape Architecture for Women, produced
some of the outstanding landscape architects of the time.
These alternative schools trained women in architecture
and landscape architecture at a time when the major university programs were closed to them, and both embraced
a collaborative approach, producing architects and landscape architects versed in both disciplines.

Throughout her career, during which she was named
dean of women landscape architects by *House and Garden*
magazine, Shipman promoted women in the field. Emerging from programs like Lowthorpe and the Cambridge
School in unprecedented numbers, young graduates encountered much resistance in a male-dominated profession. (Frederick Law Olmsted, Jr., is said to have remarked
of Beatrix Jones Farrand, fellow founding member of the
American Society of Landscape Architects, that she was
"inclined in some way to dabble in landscape architecture.") For more than 30 years Shipman employed women
landscape architects and draftswomen in her New York
City and Cornish, N.H., offices. All-female offices such as
Shipman's played a crucial role in the extraordinary success of her generation of women landscape architects, who
were routinely refused work in male-owned offices.

Shipman's work ranged from Texas to Michigan and
North Carolina to New Hampshire. Like most women
landscape architects working before the 1940s, she was seldom offered public commissions. Despite the obstacles,
however, Shipman designed several important public
projects, including Lake Shore Boulevard in Grosse Pointe,
Mich., and the Sarah Duke Memorial Garden at Duke University in Durham, N.C., both completed in the late
1930s. She is best remembered for her beautiful gardens
and estate designs. Chief among them is Rynwood (1927),

Pergola with marble columns at Wampus, estate of Mr. and Mrs. John Magee, Mount Kisco, N.Y., 1919. (Mattie Edwards Hewitt; New York State Historical Association)

Ellen Biddle Shipman. (Photograph by Bradley. *House & Garden*. © 1923, 1951.The Condé Nast Publications)

Detail from a drawing of lattice work for Mr. and Mrs. Hugh Dillman, Grosse Pointe, Mich., 1932. (Cornell University)

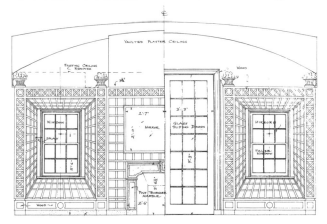

Samuel Salvage's estate in Glen Head, N.Y.; Longue Vue Gardens, the Edgar B. Stern estate in New Orleans, which Shipman designed in the late 1930s and modified over many years; and Franklin B. Lord's Cottsleigh in Syosset, N.Y., designed in the late 1920s.

Ellen Shipman was a consummate designer who left her mark on her profession, both as an advocate for a remarkable generation of women landscape architects and as a talented designer of lavish American gardens. ✍

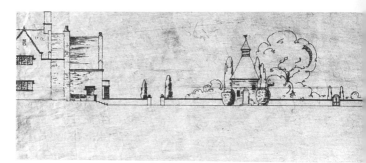

Garden sketch for Samuel A. Salvage, Rynwood, Glen Head, N.Y., 1927. (Cornell University)

Ornamental urn, estate of Mr. and Mrs. Carll Tucker, Mount Kisco, N.Y., 1947. (Cornell University)

Garden of the Misses Prynne, East Hampton, N.Y., 1924. (Nassau County Museum Reference Library)

Above: Azalea Walk, Longue Vue, 1947. Longue Vue is a rare example of an urban estate, a phenomenon seldom encountered after the 1930s. (Longue Vue House)

Center: Portico Garden and South Lawn, Longue Vue, the estate of Edgar B. and Edith Rosenwald Stern, New Orleans, 1942. (Gottscho-Schleisner; Longue Vue House)

Opposite: Mixed border, Bronx Botanical Garden, Bronx, N.Y. (Cornell University)

BEATRIX JONES FARRAND
Eleanor M. McPeck

Beatrix Jones Farrand (1872–1959), one of the finest land-scape architects of her generation, was born in New York City. She was the only child of Mary Cadwalader and Frederic Rhinelander Jones, who divorced sometime before she was 12. Given the circumstances, her early life cannot have been entirely happy, nor was it dull. Tutored at home, she often traveled abroad with her mother and her father's sister, Edith Wharton. Her uncle, John Lambert Cadwalader, a distinguished lawyer and a founder of the New York Public Library, is said to have recognized in his niece an early talent for landscape design and an "indomitable will." He later remarked, "Let her be a gardener or, for that matter, anything she wants to be. What she wishes to do will be well done."

She studied landscape briefly in Berlin and in 1893 studied landscape and horticulture for at least a year under Charles Sprague Sargent, founder and first director of the Arnold Arboretum near Boston. It was Sargent who encouraged her to become a professional. Although she later developed her own philosophy of design, she always followed Sargent's sound advice to "make the plan fit the ground and not twist the ground to fit the plan."

Following one of several European garden tours, Farrand returned to New York City and opened an office in her mother's house on East 11th Street in 1895. Working initially within the immediate circle of family friends, she received her first major commission from William Garrison of Tuxedo, N.Y., in 1896. In 1899 Jones joined 10 other distinguished practitioners to establish the American Society of Landscape Architects. She was the only woman among the founders.

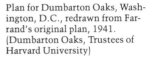

Plan for Dumbarton Oaks, Washington, D.C., redrawn from Farrand's original plan, 1941. (Dumbarton Oaks, Trustees of Harvard University)

Beatrix Jones Farrand. (Dumbarton Oaks, Trustees of Harvard University)

Opposite: Crafted gates in the herb garden, Dumbarton Oaks, c. 1950. (Dumbarton Oaks, Trustees of Harvard University)

Farrand's earliest designs were formal in character but reflected the influence of William Robinson, the English landscape architect and author of *The Wild Garden* (1881). She also admired the work of the celebrated contemporary English landscape gardener Gertrude Jekyll, who, like Robinson, advocated the use of wild and native plant materials for picturesque effect. Farrand shared with Jekyll a subtle and harmonious approach to color, based on Impressionist theory. Robert Patterson, her lifelong associate, later wrote that Farrand's work had a "freedom of scale, a subtle softness of line and an unobtrusive asymmetry." Her designs combined horticultural impressionism and the best elements of formal English landscape gardening.

Unfortunately, none of Jones's earliest gardens survives, although some evidence of her approach may be gleaned from drawings preserved at the University of California. Several important projects, including the country estate (1914–32) of Willard Straight in Old Westbury, Long Island, N.Y., have been destroyed. The town garden (1913–43) for J. Pierpont Morgan in New York City survives in only fragmentary form. One of Farrand's most successful gardens (1925–50), designed for Abby Aldrich Rockefeller in Seal Harbor, Maine, is still well maintained by the Rockefeller family.

Dumbarton Oaks in Washington, D.C., is Farrand's finest surviving work. Beginning in 1921 and over the next 26 years, Farrand transformed for her clients Mildred and Robert Woods Bliss what had been a farm into one of the most imaginative gardens in this country. The entire composition reflects her clear understanding of the topographic subtleties of the site. Lending complexity to the whole is

the principle of asymmetry. The formal Georgian house
was placed deliberately off axis, with its principal terraces
extending to the east and descending to informal wooded
areas below. Often when resolution is expected, a sudden
turn in the walk leads to some unseen arbor, some unantic-
ipated part of the garden. Dumbarton Oaks is everywhere
marked by a richness of architectural detail, an imaginative
choice of materials and delicacy and restraint—qualities associated with all of Farrand's best work.

Among her private clients Farrand gained a reputation
for thoroughness and certainty of approach. This reputation also extended to her campus work. Beginning in 1916
she designed the graduate college gardens at Princeton University. At Yale University between 1922 and 1945 she designed the Memorial Quadrangle, Silliman College Quadrangle and the Marsh Botanical Garden. Farrand's other
campus commissions include those for the University of
Chicago (1929–36) and Vassar (1926–27), Hamilton (1924)
and Oberlin (1939–46) colleges.

Farrand devoted her final years to the creation of Reef
Point Gardens in Bar Harbor, Maine, which she and her
husband had begun in 1945. Designed for both scholarly
and experimental purposes, the project ultimately included
a test garden of native flora, an extensive library and an
herbarium. In 1955, concerned about the survival of Reef
Point, Farrand transferred the library, the herbarium and
her personal correspondence to the University of California
at Berkeley. 🌿

Opposite: Swimming pool and loggia, Dumbarton Oaks, c. 1940. (Dumbarton Oaks, Trustees of Harvard University)

Orchard in the lower garden, Dumbarton Oaks, c. 1950. (Dumbarton Oaks, Trustees of Harvard University)

Rose garden looking west to the orangery, Dumbarton Oaks, c. 1950. (Dumbarton Oaks, Trustees of Harvard University)

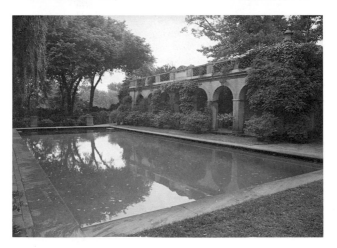

Sketch for grounds of the William R. Garrison estate, Tuxedo, N.Y., 1896. (Environmental Design, University of California, Berkeley)

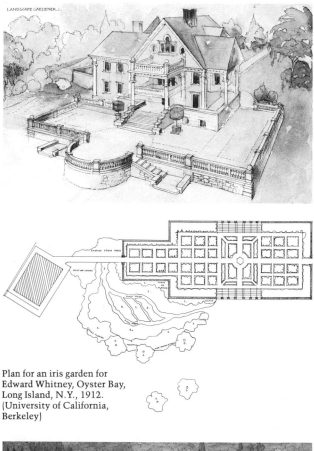

Plan for an iris garden for Edward Whitney, Oyster Bay, Long Island, N.Y., 1912. (University of California, Berkeley)

Sketch of a garden for Willard Straight, Old Westbury, Long Island, N.Y., 1914, possibly by an assistant to Farrand. (University of California, Berkeley)

Opposite: Silliman College, Yale University. (*Yale Alumni News*, September 27, 1940)

Below and center: Spirit Walk and pool, Abby Aldrich Rockefeller garden, Seal Harbor, Maine. (© 1960 Ezra Stoller)

FRANK ALBERT WAUGH
Frederick R. Steiner

Throughout his life, Frank Albert Waugh (1869–1943) remained committed to three ideals: designing comfortable and attractive suburban homes; planning clean, healthful, convenient and beautiful cities; and protecting and interpreting the native landscape. These ideals were reflected in his work as an educator, writer and practitioner.

Waugh was born on a farm in Sheboygan Falls, Wis., and grew up in McPherson County, Kans. He received his undergraduate degree from Kansas State Agricultural College (now Kansas State University) in 1891. A year later, he was appointed professor of horticulture at the Oklahoma Agricultural and Mechanical College (now Oklahoma State University). While teaching there, he simultaneously completed his studies for a Master of Science degree in horticulture and botany from Kansas State Agricultural College in 1894. Waugh's thesis presented a master plan for the development of grounds and plantings on the Oklahoma campus that included recommendations for the organization and layout of buildings, walkways, demonstration plots and plantings. He later did additional graduate work at Cornell University, took special courses in landscape design at the Gaertnerlehranstalt zu Dahlen in Germany and studied etching at the Ecole des Beaux Arts in Paris.

Waugh was appointed professor of horticulture at the University of Vermont in 1895. In 1902 he became professor of horticulture and landscape gardening at Massachusetts State Agricultural College (now the University of Massachusetts), where he established the Department of Landscape Gardening, later renamed the Department of Landscape Architecture. Waugh remained there until his retirement in 1939. For many years, he was head of both the Department of Landscape Architecture and the larger Division of Horticulture, which also included departments of pomology, floriculture, vegetable gardening and forestry. As an educator, he bridged the landscape gardening tradition of the 19th century and the growing professionalism in landscape architecture during the 20th century. Several of his former students pursued careers in education, teaching in or developing new programs in landscape architecture.

A prolific writer, Waugh published eight books as well as numerous articles and extension bulletins on the topics of landscape gardening, architecture and planning. His book *Landscape Gardening* (1899) was used as a textbook throughout the country. He was also responsible for editing and revising Andrew Jackson Downing's *Landscape Gardening* in 1921. Additional publications were produced on a wide variety of agricultural topics ranging from orchard management to home pork production. While maintaining his agricultural interests, however, Waugh remained committed to the arts, especially photography and music.

Although principally an academic, Waugh also was a practitioner. In 1914 he prepared a 50-year master plan for Kansas State College. He was especially active undertaking varied efforts with the Massachusetts Cooperative Extension Service. During several summers he prepared plans and reports about recreational developments for the U.S. Forest Service. Among his most notable projects were the 1918 town plan of Grand Canyon Village in Arizona and the 1920 design of the famous scenic drive encircling Mt. Hood in Oregon. Waugh was also involved in the design and maintenance of the University of Massachusetts campus, where he implemented and furthered the recommendations made by Frederick Law Olmsted and Warren H. Manning. 🐾

Frank Albert Waugh playing the flute, 1926. (University of Massachusetts)

Section of Mt. Hood's scenic drive. Waugh continued to serve as an adviser on Mt. Hood's development after the drive's completion. (Oregon Historical Society)

Opposite and below: Waugh's home in Amherst, Mass., and its grounds plan. (University of Massachusetts)

Etching of beech trees and rocks by Waugh, who maintained a long-term interest in the arts. (University of Massachusetts)

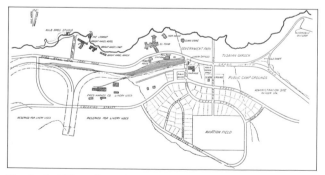

Plan for the Village of Grand Canyon, Ariz., 1918, for the U.S. Forest Service.

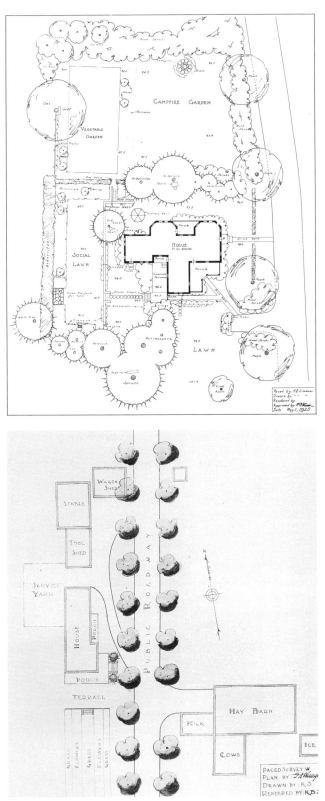

Farmstead plan for the Barclay farm, Paxton, Mass. Waugh's work with the agricultural program of the University of Massachusetts led to the development of private farm plans such as this. (University of Massachusetts)

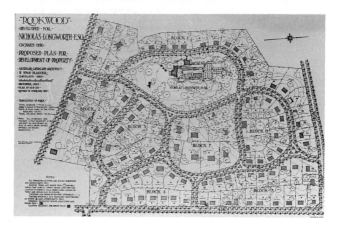

ALBERT DAVIS TAYLOR
Noël Dorsey Vernon

Through his practice and professional service, Albert Davis Taylor (1883–1951) became a leader in the profession of landscape architecture from the early 1920s until his death in 1951. Born in Carlisle, Mass., he attended Massachusetts State Agricultural College (now the University of Massachusetts) and Boston College, receiving his S.B. and A.B. degrees in 1905. Enrolling at Cornell University, Taylor studied under Liberty Hyde Bailey and Olmsted protégé Bryant Fleming, receiving a master's degree from the College of Agriculture in 1906.

He remained in Ithaca, N.Y., for two additional years, teaching in the landscape architecture program and rounding out his education with a tour of Europe in the summer of 1907. Taylor then worked for Warren H. Manning as a draftsman. Because Manning had trained with Frederick Law Olmsted, Taylor soon became even more well grounded in the tradition of the Olmsteds. In 1912, four years after he joined the Manning firm, Taylor became an associate.

In 1913 Taylor opened his own firm in Cleveland, which involved him in a wide range of projects. Taylor's estate design work generally combined a naturalistic park perimeter with some degree of formal garden and terrace treatment near the house—an early 20th-century approach typical of many East Coast landscape architects. Major examples of Taylor's estate and planting design included the W. H. Knoll estate (1919) in Fort Wayne, Ind., and the W. H. Albers (1925) and Julius Fleishman (1926) estates in Cincinnati. The latter two were part of a larger luxury subdivision called Camargo (now the Village of Indian Hill), which Taylor laid out in 1925. For Nicholas Longworth he also had designed an earlier Cincinnati suburb, Rookwood (1922), which took full advantage of Taylor's knowledge of Olmstedian subdivision design.

Taylor's government work included the Pentagon site plan (1942) outside Washington, D.C., as well as several major defense housing projects. His most noted park project was the plan for Forest Hill Park in East Cleveland and Cleveland Heights, Ohio, for which Taylor produced an extensive report in 1938. Once a Rockefeller estate, the park included the requisite great meadow, wooded rambles and lake in the manner of Central and Prospect parks. In-

Opposite: Plan for Rookwood,
a subdivision of Nicholas
Longworth's Cincinnati estate,
1922. (*Architecture and Design*,
1937)

Albert Davis Taylor. (*Landscape
Architecture*)

THE TEA HOUSE.
DAISY HILL FARMS

Center and above: Sketch for the tea house and pool of O. P. and M. J.
Van Sweringen's Daisy Hill Farms, 1925, Chagrin Falls, Ohio, and the
landscape at maturity, c. 1935. (*Architecture and Design*, 1937)

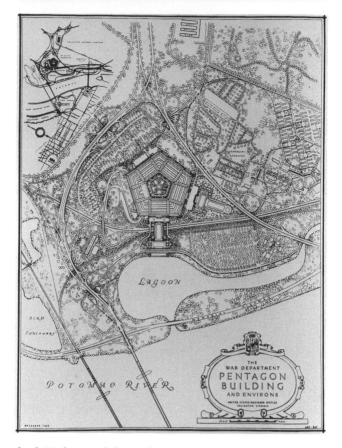

deed, Taylor cited these Olmsted and Vaux designs as important examples in his report. Taylor's masterly use of the existing terrain and circulation systems at Forest Hill Park, however, indicated that he was far more than a copyist.

With the exception of preprofessionals such as Adolph Strauch, Taylor was one of the first landscape architects to practice in Ohio. His Cleveland office served as a training ground for generations of noted landscape architects. Chief among these were his office mainstays, Gordon D. Cooper and Herbert L. Flint. Flint, who also trained with the Manning firm and at Cornell, worked with Taylor in Cleveland from 1916 until 1921, when he was sent to Orlando, Fla., to run a second office. Eleanor Christie, a Lowthorpe School graduate, designed the office's planting plans in the early 1920s and helped Taylor and Cooper with their book, *The Complete Garden* (1921). Taylor and his colleagues also prepared more than 40 editions of "Construction Notes" published in *Landscape Architecture* between 1922 and 1936.

Taylor's leadership abilities and concern for the profession led him to serve as president of the American Society of Landscape Architects from 1935 to 1940. His determination, his sense of justice and his egalitarian aims for the once-elitist American Society of Landscape Architects did much to broaden its membership and image. Taylor's tireless fight for the cause of landscape architecture—as well as the aesthetic and technical quality of his built work—earned him his well-deserved national reputation. 🍂

Opposite: Plan for the site of the Pentagon, Arlington, Va., outside Washington, D.C., 1942. (*Architecture and Design*, 1937)

Maple Grove Park, near Windham, Ohio, a pre–World War II defense housing project. (*Architecture and Design*, 1937)

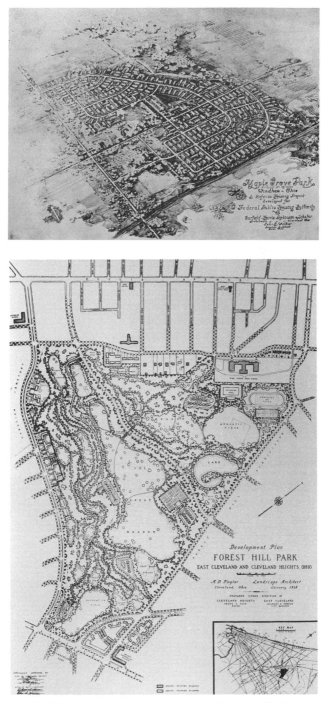

Forest Hill Park, a recreational area created from land owned by Cleveland and East Cleveland. The park retains many of the original features of the Taylor plan. (*Architecture and Design*, 1937)

ELBERT PEETS
Paul D. Spreiregen

Educated as a landscape architect and accomplished as a practitioner, Elbert Peets's principal contributions were in the fields of town planning and urban design. It was not an unusual direction for a landscape architect of his time.Like Andrew Jackson Downing and Frederick Law Olmsted before him, he helped establish his century's foundations for planning as a recognized discipline. The chief opportunities lay in the design of residential and industrial communities and the improvement of cities—including parks, civic centers, campuses and roadway systems.

Peets (1886–1968) was born in Hudson, Ohio. A brilliant student, he gained experience in practical landscape work before earning his degree in landscape architecture at Harvard University in 1915. He then assisted the noted German planner Werner Hegemann in designing Kohler, Wis. (1916). During World War I Peets designed military facilities, resuming community design work with Hegemann after the war. Their collaboration continued until Hegemann's death in 1936. By then, Peets's interest in town planning was clearly established.

A year in Europe from 1920 to 1921 as a Charles Eliot Traveling Fellow fueled his intellect and sparked his vision. Unlike many who were similarly directed, Peets perceived the underlying principles of past city design and their applicability to the cities of his own time.

Returning to the United States, he and Hegemann completed two landmark efforts—Wyomissing Park (1917–21), a residential extension of Reading, Pa., and a book, *Civic Art: The American Vitruvius* (1922). Wyomissing Park remains a model residential community serving a broad population spectrum. With more than 1,000 of Peets's drawings, *Civic Art* stands as a compendium of classic dimension. Peets continued to write on town planning for the next 40 years, illustrating his essays with telling sketches.

Peets practiced in Cleveland from 1923 to 1933, the period during which he wrote some of his best essays—on the great town planners of history, on Pierre Charles L'Enfant

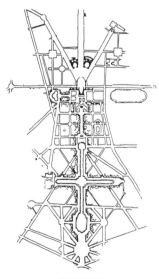

VERSAILLES

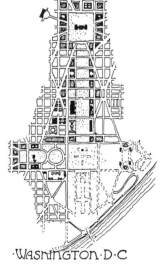

·Washington·D·C

Elbert Peets. (Cornell University)

Plan for refining central Washington, D.C. (*Architectural Record*, September 1932)

t· THEATER
u· SUPREME COURT BUILDING
v,v· "GRAND FOUNTAINS"
w· NATIONAL CHURCH
xx· "STATUES, COLUMNS, OR OBELISKS"
y· ESPLANADE: DESIGN UNCERTAIN, BUT APPARENTLY INTENDED TO BE AN OPEN PLAZA, NOT A PARK

EAST
NORTH ← → SOUTH
WEST

AXIS C IS EQUIDISTANT FROM AXES A & D. AXIS B MARKS A THIRD OF THE DISTANCE FROM A TO D.

THIS IS A RECONSTRUCTION OF L'ENFANT'S DESIGN FOR THE CENTRAL PART OF WASHINGTON, BASED ON HIS PLAN & REPORTS. Elbert Peets, 1928

SCALE, 1 INCH EQUALS 660 FEET
COPYRIGHT 1932 THE ARCHITECTURAL RECORD

a· UPPER CAPITOL SQUARE WITH ARCADES
b· CAPITOL
c· LOWER CAPITOL SQUARE
d· CASCADE
e· CANAL
f· MARKET & CANAL PORT
g· RESIDENCES OF FOREIGN MINISTERS, ETC., WITH GARDENS
h· "GRAND AVENUE"
i· NAVAL ITINERARY & MEMORIAL COLUMN

POTOMAC RIVER

j· VIEW DOWN RIVER
AVENUE 150 FEET WIDE, TAPERING TO 100 FEET
k· PUBLIC PARK?
l· LAWN 400 FEET WIDE
m· EQUESTRIAN STATUE or GEORGE WASHINGTON
n· LANDING QUAY?
o· FOUNTAIN
p· PRESIDENT'S HOUSE ("WHITE HOUSE")
q,q· VISTAS FROM PRESIDENT'S HOUSE
r,r· EXECUTIVE DEPARTMENT BUILDINGS
s,s· GARDENS OF PRESIDENT'S HOUSE?

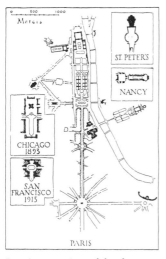

Peets's comparison of the plans for Versailles, Washington, D.C., and Paris.

Original plan for Greendale, Wis., 1938. The north-south axis, Broad Street, meets the east-west Northway at the civic center.

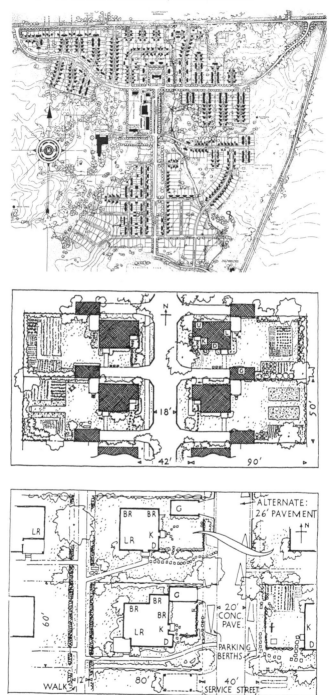

Center and above: Siting plan for single-family houses, Greendale.

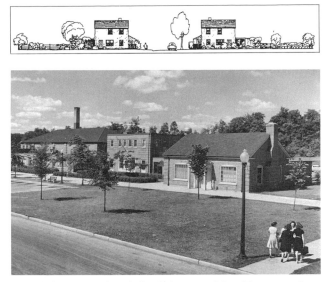

Top and above: Typical single-family houses and Broad Street near the post office, Greendale, c. 1938. (Cornell University)

and the planning of Washington, D.C. The Depression brought him to Washington, where he developed the design for Greendale, Wis. (1938). Of the three Greenbelt towns, this was the best planned and the best executed. It and Wyomissing Park stand as Peets's most exemplary realizations. Other work during this period included preparing plans for Santa Catalina Island in California and Puerto Rico. During World War II he again worked on war-related housing and planning projects.

After World War II, his reputation well established, Peets designed the new residential community of Park Forest, Ill. (1946–47), and an extension to Greendale (1950). With Washington architect Louis Justement, he proposed a prophetic plan for the much-photographed slum area of southwest Washington, D.C. Instead of razing it through urban renewal, Peets would have restored the area, preserving the kind of neighborhood character found in nearby Georgetown and Capitol Hill. During the 1950s Peets taught at Harvard and Yale universities and served on the U.S. Commission of Fine Arts. A collection of his illustrated essays was published in 1968, the year he died at age 82.

Peets's near half-century career embraced two important movements in American urban design—the turn-of-the-century City Beautiful movement to the 1960s urban design eras. In addition, his career embraced five significant periods of American residential design—World War I housing, the private developments of the 1920s, the federally sponsored work of the 1930s, World War II housing and postwar, socially oriented communities. Because town planning as an activity is so irregular in this country, only a portion of Peets's plans has been realized, let alone widely influential. The legacy of his essays and drawings is partial compensation. In them lies the guidance that future generations would do well to seek. 🐾

THOMAS CHURCH
David C. Streatfield

Thomas Church (1902–78) transformed landscape design from the manipulation of an eclectic range of styles dependent on past models to a completely modern design mode. His influence was considerable, especially in the area in which he excelled—gardens. His garden designs not only exhibited a full range of solutions but also explored the artistic use of new materials and retained the traditional concern for fine craftsmanship; his widely read articles and books demonstrated his design principles to a broad lay and professional audience; and a number of his assistants subsequently became prominent landscape architects in their own right: Garrett Eckbo, Lawrence Halprin, Douglas Baylis and Robert Royston.

Born in Boston, Church grew up in the San Francisco Bay area. He studied landscape architecture at the University of California, Berkeley, and at Harvard University. After graduation he traveled through Europe to study how Mediterranean garden traditions could be adapted in California. In 1929 he opened his first office in Pasatiempo, Calif., where he designed a series of small gardens for weekend use.

The vastly changed social and economic conditions of the Depression forced Church to develop a new mode of garden design and to move to San Francisco in 1932. He treated the garden as an outdoor living room—one element of a spatial continuum that included the house. The use of extensive areas of paving, mowed trim slabs, ground covers and clipped evergreen hedges helped reduce maintenance costs. Existing trees were retained as sculptural counterpoints. He used these devices to create simplified versions of geometric garden styles, principally based on baroque gardens of 17th-century France.

Dewey Donnell residence (1948), Sonoma, Calif., evoking the winding character of the salt marshes below and the lines of the pool's sculpture. (David Streatfield; Thomas Church)

Thomas Church. (© Carolyn Caddes)

Low-maintenance materials on a "living" terrace, Hervey Parke Clark residence (1936), Woodside, Calif. (Thomas Church)

After Church traveled to Finland to meet Alvar Aalto in 1937, a new dynamic asymmetry incorporating a fluid use of curved forms appeared in his work. This was also the result of his close collaboration with modern artists such as Florence Allston Swift and Adaline Kent. By the end of the 1930s, Church's designs had become completely abstract and were designed to produce a visual endlessness with a multiplicity of visual foci. His work is especially notable for the masterly way in which he drew both from historical precedents without slavishly copying them and from nonrepresentational forms of modern art. The finest example of this fluid abstract manner can be found at the Dewey Donnell garden (1948) in Sonoma, Calif.

Church's later approach to design was humanistic and flexible in nature. His designs have an inevitability that reflects his abhorrence of stylistic absolutism. Because the character of the architecture, the site and the way in which the client wished to live determined the design solution, Church produced a considerable range of design solutions in more than 2,000 garden plans between 1929 and 1976. These designs embraced naturalistic, abstract and symmetrical forms. This range of forms was achieved with masterly understatement, unlike the work of many of his younger contemporaries. By the 1960s, however, his work was marked by a return to symmetrical forms.

In addition to his private California residential work, the chief basis for his reputation, he was the landscape architect for the University of California campuses at Berkeley and Santa Cruz and for Stanford University. His work at this larger scale was sometimes less assured. His most successful large-scale design was the Technical Center (1956) for the General Motors Corporation in Detroit. In addition, he did work at Longwood Gardens (1971–74) in Delaware and at the headquarters (1962) of *Sunset* magazine in Menlo Park, Calif. ✥

Opposite: Pardee Erdman residence (1964), Montecito, Calif., exemplifying a return to symmetrical forms.

Below: Formal plaza, Stanford
University (1960), Palo Alto,
Calif.

Center: Alice Erving residence
(1953), Montecito, Calif. (Roy
Flamm, Bancroft Library)

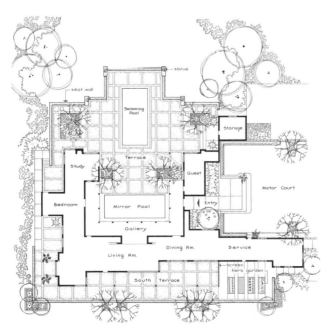

CAMPUSES
Richard P. Dober

Campus as landscape—it is an evocative phrase, conjuring up open spaces, trees and gardens. In the United States there are more than 3,300 such splendid settings for architecture serving higher education. Pleasant places to visit, these art forms give three-dimensional evidence of changing fashions and perceptions about greenery planted and organized for functional, visual and symbolic effect. Coast to coast, the landscape architect's work is visible, from Frederick Law Olmsted's delineating designs for Stanford University to Warren H. Manning's shaping of Amherst College's hilltop location, with its now-treasured vistas.

The extraordinary range in campus type, extent and use of landcape reflects climate, acreage available and cultural values. America's first colleges, Harvard, Yale and Brown, each more than two centuries old, began with modest greens and yards, as did coeval Dartmouth and Princeton. The first three institutions became embedded in dense urbanization. Their landscapes evolved, constrained by limited land ownership, while Dartmouth and Princeton were extended generously into their rural surroundings. One approaches and moves through the campuses sensing these essential differences.

The second wave of college founding, through the Civil War, continued and extended the colonial aesthetic: greenswards, tree-lined walkways, buildings and plantings situated in space, rather than enclosing space—thus, Bowdoin in Maine, Dickinson in Pennsylvania, Davidson in North Carolina and Wittenberg in Ohio. Their archetype fully realized is Mount Holyoke College in Massachusetts. Founded in 1837, the college grounds now number 800 acres and include four quadrangles overlooking a small lake and, beyond the Prospect Hills, woodlands, bridle trails, running paths, an arboretum and a wildlife sanctuary. Memorial gardens, playfields and flowering species announce the passing seasons.

Contrast these informal campus designs with the studied arrangement of the first buildings and landscapes at the College of William and Mary (1695), which balances the Governor's Palace at the other end of Williamsburg's Duke of Gloucester Street; Joseph Jacques Ramée's courtyard scheme for Union College (1795) in Schenectady, N.Y.; and Thomas Jefferson's masterwork at the University of Vir-

Opposite: Grounds of Stanford
University (1886–91, Frederick
Law Olmsted), Palo Alto, Calif.,
designed in a formal symmetrical
pattern. (Stanford University)

Entrance gate to Campus Green,
Brown University, Providence, a
more traditional threshold to a
campus open space. (Richard P.
Dober)

Central campus arcade, Stanford University, a Romanesque gateway to
an open area. (Richard P. Dober)

ginia (1817–26), where buildings, paths, walls and gardens,
ensemble, unify site and structures.

Distinctive landscapes help create a sense of place: the
informality of the original Radcliffe Quadrangle versus the
urbanity of the Massachusetts Institute of Technology's
east campus, a strongly shaped open space punctuated by
Alexander Calder's heroic mobile; the ravine and rhodo-
dendron collection at the base of Bentley Hall at Allegheny
College (1815), Meadville, Pa., versus the mannerly sculpture garden at the University of California, Los Angeles
(1881). The rose collection at Swarthmore College (1864)
in Pennsylvania and the enchanting Sarah Duke flower
beddings at Duke University (1838) in North Carolina provide tranquil enclaves near busy central campuses.

The rise of the modern university in the mid-19th century brought about formal designs, inspired by magisterial,
if not romantic, interpretations of Gothic, Georgian and
classical architecture. Monumental enclosing quadrangles
can be found at Ohio State University (1870), the University of Chicago (1891) and Southern Methodist University
(1910). Typically, the concept includes a visually commanding building and open space, a stage for campus life,
as evident in landscape architect A. T. Erwin's seminal design in 1892 for Iowa State University.

Trees and ground covers subtly proclaim regional differences, a cherished campus design tradition from Frederick
Law Olmsted and his work at Stanford (1885) to anony-
mous groundskeepers. Simpson College (1860), Indianola
Iowa, was laid out to look like an urban park, a civilizing
gesture amid prairie and farmland. Its silver maples became a regional landmark. The University of Miami campus (1925) is wrapped around an artificial lake, the rim
planted with palms, a land developer's vision of a campus
appropriate for tropical Florida. At Pomona College in California, Ralph Cornell in 1945 used architecture as an arma-
ture for an extraordinary sequence of plant materials and
campus open spaces. The insertion of the University of
California at Santa Cruz (1963) into a redwood forest, inspired by Thomas Church's sensitive terrain analysis, epit-
omizes the melding of nature discovered or adapted for a
campus design image.

All campuses are truly pedestrian precincts, providing
special opportunities to experience the intertwining of architecture and landscape, which, for historical interest or
aesthetic enjoyment, are well worth a detour in any
journey. 🌿

Massachusetts Institute of Technology, East Campus, Cambridge, Mass.,
a contemporary version of a formal, neoclassical campus design.
(Richard P. Dober)

Radcliffe College, Cambridge,
Mass., where lawns, trees and
buildings shape a less formal green
space in one of America's oldest
and densest urban areas. (Richard
P. Dober)

Opposite center: Central campus,
University of New Mexico, Albuquerque, a stark landscape reflecting an arid climate. (Richard P.
Dober)

Opposite: Main campus, Bowdoin
College, Brunswick, Maine, with
deciduous trees and greenswards,
a conventional campus design pal-
ette for the Northeast. (Richard P.
Dober)

Gazebo and pond, Wheaton College, Norton, Mass., a more intimate
landscape setting for individual or group enjoyment. (Richard P. Dober)

Chapel, Mount Auburn (1845, 1854, Jacob Bigelow), Boston, constructed of Quincy granite. (© 1976 Alan Ward)

Plan for Mount Auburn, 1845. (Walter, *Mount Auburn Illustrated*, 1847)

Consecration Dell, Mount Auburn, an area preserving the original landscape of the "rural" cemetery. (© 1977 Alan Ward)

Washington Tower (1855, Jacob Bigelow), Mount Auburn, overlooking the Charles River. (© 1981 Alan Ward)

CEMETERIES
Blanche Linden-Ward

Long before the professionalization of landscape architecture, new American cemeteries provided models of landscape taste and trained generations of landscape designers, producing lasting effects on our built environment. By the mid-19th century the popularity of cemeteries as tourist attractions and "pleasure grounds" signaled a demand for public parks, according to New York art critic Clarence Cook, who in 1869 agreed with Andrew Jackson Downing that cemeteries were "all the rage." They were "famous over the whole country and thousands of people visited them annually."

America's first designed funerary landscape, quite unlike traditional barren graveyards and churchyards, was New Haven's New Burying Ground (later Grove Street Cemetery), founded in 1796 by James Hillhouse and laid out by Josiah Meigs. Its gridded avenues, lined by columnar poplars on a flat six-acre site, reflects more the constitutional era's rationalism than the romanticism that four decades later produced picturesque "rural" cemeteries on extensive tracts of dramatic suburban land with hills, dales, woods, ponds and symbolic river vistas.

In 1831 the Massachusetts Horticultural Society created Boston's Mount Auburn, the first "rural" cemetery and prototype for many others. Gen. Henry A. S. Dearborn designed its original 72 acres based on the model of Père Lachaise in Paris. Dr. Jacob Bigelow was responsible for Mount Auburn's Egyptian gate, Gothic chapel and Norman tower, inspired by structures in English gardens; and as president from 1845 to 1871, he guided landscape change from the picturesque to the gardenesque, removing woods, introducing ornamental plantings and transforming Mount Auburn into a garden cemetery.

John Jay Smith, Downing's successor as editor of *The Horticulturist*, organized Philadelphia's 20-acre Laurel Hill in 1836. The landscape design by architect John Notman was tighter and more geometric than Mount Auburn's winding roads and paths. His plan fit the smaller, flatter site high above the Schuylkill River. In 1848 Notman also laid out the 45-acre Holly-Wood Cemetery with views of Richmond, Va., across the James River.

Brooklyn real estate developer Henry E. Pierrepont chose a 178-acre site for Green-Wood in 1838. Civil engineer Maj. David B. Douglass designed its six lakes, 22 miles of roads and 30 miles of paths. Within a decade, Zebedee Cook, who had helped found Mount Auburn, and Almerin Hotchkiss, recently selected as cemetery superintendent, expanded Green-Wood's landscape to 478 acres with rustic Tuscan and Gothic structures by Richard Upjohn and his son, Richard M. Upjohn. In 1848 Hotchkiss left for St. Louis to develop Bellefontaine Cemetery overlooking the Mississippi River.

Cincinnati horticulturists established Spring Grove in 1845 with designs by local architect Howard Daniels. This commission launched Daniels's career, during which he produced a dozen cemeteries, a fourth-place entry in the Central Park design competition and Baltimore's Druid Hill Park. Prussian landscape gardener Adolph Strauch, a student of European park reformer Prince Pückler-Muskau, became superintendent in 1855. His "landscape lawn plan" eliminated cluttering fences and medium-sized

stones and structured ornamental plantings to frame
spreading lawns, lakes and monuments in order to create
vistas. Strauch formalized the taste for the beautiful, influencing cemetery design and redesign for more than half a
century.

Unlike his contemporaries, Frederick Law Olmsted argued that cemeteries should not resemble "pleasure
grounds" or double as recreational pursuits. His Mountain
View Cemetery (1865) in Oakland, Calif., unlike his parks
and suburbs, has the severe linearity of straight roads further defined by hedges and walls. It had little effect on either subsequent cemetery design or its own later additions.

The first national cemeteries modified the landscape
lawn plan. William Saunders laid out a 17-acre Union
burial area in 1863 next to the decade-old "rural" cemetery
of the town of Gettysburg, Pa.; and Arlington National
Cemetery was created the next year on the old Robert E.
Lee estate across the Potomac River from Washington,
D.C.

Landscape architect H. W. S. Cleveland and architect
William Le Baron Jenny followed the "rural" model for
Chicago's Graceland (1860). But when O. C. Simonds assumed management in 1883, he established himself as a
national advocate of Strauch's landscape lawn plan, ac-
claimed internationally as the "American system."

Opposite: Doric entrance and
Gothic chapel, Laurel Hill, designed by Notman. These features
appealed especially to those who
considered the Egyptian style
"heathen" and "un-American."
(© 1980 Alan Ward)

Simonds founded the Association of American Cemetery Superintendents in 1887, addressing newly professionalized "cemeterians" through F. J. Haight's *Modern Cemetery* (1890), renamed *Park and Cemetery* in 1895.

Forest Lawn Cemetery (1906) near Los Angeles hired Dr. Hubert Eaton in 1916 to fashion a highly planned and regulated memorial park, expanded to more than 1,200 acres on four sites. Henceforth, cemetery professionals, rather than landscape architects or gentleman trustees interested in horticulture, provided most cemetery design and redesign based primarily on economic considerations, using the memorial park concept or the even plainer, more efficient and purely functional lawn plan, which permitted only modest plaques set almost invisibly in well-manicured sod.

Most American cemeteries created in the 20th century are profit-making ventures, unlike the older, quasi-public "rural" or "garden" cemeteries, which had many more civic and cultural functions than simply burial of the dead. Still, the major examples of the "rural" cemetery movement remain intact as important romantic landscapes, although often they have been expanded and altered by subsequent periods of changing taste and the wear and tear of time. Many of them merit the attention of preservationists as historic places based on design significance alone. ✑

Plan for Laurel Hill, Philadelphia, 1836, designed by John Notman and inspired by Kensal Green Cemetery, London. (© 1980 Alan Ward)

Strollers at Laurel Hill, with the Schuylkill River in the background. (*Godey's Lady's Book*, 1844)

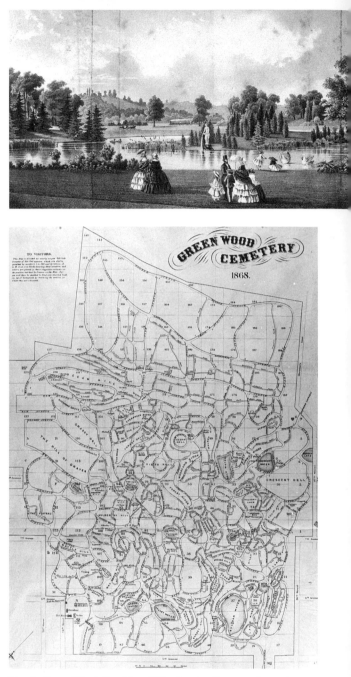

Plan for Green-Wood, Brooklyn, N.Y., showing the expansion under
Almerin Hotchkiss. (© 1980 Alan Ward)

Opposite: Entrance gates opening
to the Heron Fountain at Forest
Lawn, Glendale, Calif. (Forest
Lawn Cemetery)

Geyser Lake at Spring Grove, Cincinnati, part of Adolph Strauch's 1857 "landscape lawn plan." (© 1983 Alan Ward)

Forest Lawn, an example of a memorial park with a functional lawn plan. (Forest Lawn Cemetery)

CITY PLANNING
Lance M. Neckar

Landscape architects had a seminal role in the development of city planning in the United States. Many landscape architects would date the involvement of their profession in city planning from the turn of the century, citing the role of Frederick Law Olmsted, Jr., as a member of the McMillan Commission, which set about to redesign Washington, D.C., in 1901. Others would turn to the older Olmsted's plan for the 1893 World's Columbian Exposition in Chicago. However, the urban planning role of landscape architects goes back even further. Olmsted and Vaux's design of Central Park in New York City in 1858 and the subsequent development of urban park systems in the late 19th and early 20th centuries provided significant concepts for urban growth. The mid-19th-century suburban town designs by Olmsted, Jed Hotchkiss, H. W. S. Cleveland and others constituted the first organized visions of urbanization.

The primary impetus for creating the discipline and profession of city planning came in the decades following the McMillan Plan. This was the era of the City Beautiful, a phrase coined by Charles Mulford Robinson, a journalist-turned-planner and author of the influential *Modern Civic Art, or the City Made Beautiful* (1903). Most projects were executed by landscape architects and architects. The ideal of these early plans was embodied in the civic center, a monumental space designed for city government buildings. Ideally, this civic center, by its location and grandeur, would symbolize the improvement of the whole city. Many landscape architects also provided schematic park system, waterfront and suburban subdivision plans as a regular component of their services.

While Robinson and Daniel H. Burnham were arguably the most famous planners of the day, landscape architects were the preeminent organizers of the profession of city planning. In 1909 the first national conference on city planning was held, with the younger Olmsted and John Nolen making significant presentations. That year Nolen persuaded Wisconsin's legislature to adopt the first legislation authorizing cities to create planning commissions and prepare city plans. That same year, James S. Pray offered the first course in city planning at Harvard University's School of Landscape Architecture.

Opposite: World's Columbian Exposition, a turn-of-the-century model for making cities more beautiful. (Neckar collection)

Brattle Street, Cambridge, Mass., c. 1900, an archetype of city street design. (Minneapolis Public Library)

THE McMILLAN PLAN, 1901

LEGEND:

AREAS PROPOSED FOR PARKS AND PUBLIC BUILDINGS

RELATED FACILITIES OPEN TO THE PUBLIC

WATERFRONT DRIVES

The McMillan Plan of 1901 for Washington, D.C., which provided landscape architects with a key early role in city planning. (National Capital Planning Commission)

Plan for the bay front and esplanade, San Diego, 1907, by John
Nolen, who had a passion for waterfront development. (Harvard
University)

Riverfront, Budapest, Hungary,
one of several European cities
much admired for their riverfront
designs. (Minneapolis Public Library)

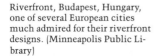

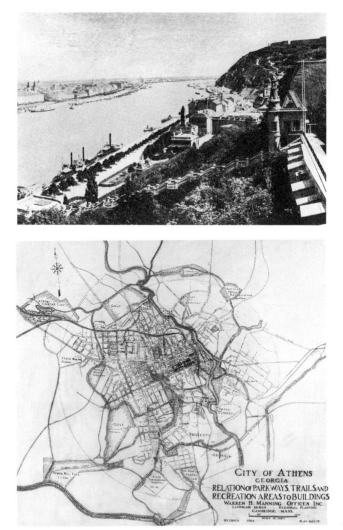

Plan by Warren H. Manning for Athens, Ga., 1924, a typical land
resource-oriented design linking riverfront parks and botanical gardens.
(Iowa State University)

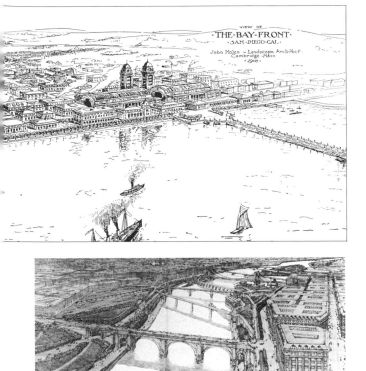

Plan for Minneapolis, 1917, by E. H. Bennett. Although not a landscape architect, Bennett was influenced by H. W. S. Cleveland, as seen here in the special attention given to the Mississippi riverfront. (Minneapolis Public Library)

By the decade's end the grandeur of the City Beautiful had paled, and planners began examining the social, economic and functional aspects of the city. Again, landscape architects were among the first to try "scientific" processes. Frederick Law Olmsted, Jr., attempted to incorporate statistical analysis in his report to the Civic Improvement Committee of New Haven in 1910. Warren H. Manning, taking an entirely different tack, examined landscape resources such as forest cover and soil in his planning work of the same period for Billerica, Mass.

Science contributed to the growth of professionalism. It was becoming clear that no single established profession could plan a city alone. By 1915, 14 landscape architects took the lead among other professions in establishing the American City Planning Institute, now the American Planning Association. Harvard in 1923 offered a city planning option in landscape architecture and in 1929, under Henry V. Hubbard's leadership, created the first separate School of City Planning.

In the 1920s and 1930s, the notion of interdisciplinary planning was emphasized in designing industrial and residential communities; landscape architects were cast as leaders or participants in many teams. As the discipline and profession of planning gained strength and legislative support in subsequent decades, many landscape architects turned to government employment or became consultants in urban landscape design, and the growth of several prominent firms in practice today can be traced to this specialization. ✍

Plan for Middleton Place, outside Charleston, S.C. (Lockwood, *Gardens of Colony and State*, 1934)

Terracing at Middleton Place leading down to the floodplain. (Middleton Place)

Mount Vernon, where garden design principles were applied to a working farm. (Lockwood)

Biltmore, Asheville, N.C., 1900, a product of the Olmsted firm with an elaborate formal garden in the foreground. (George R. King)

COUNTRY ESTATES
Malcolm Cairns

Derived from French Renaissance chateaux, Italian villas and English country homes, American country estates dot the outskirts of most major cities. The landscapes surrounding these symbols of wealth, either singularly as at Biltmore, San Simeon and Vizcaya, or collectively in "Gold Coast" enclaves like Newport, Lake Forest and Tuxedo Park, are synonymous with suburban luxury, spaciousness and design opulence. At their best, they represent a marriage of house and garden, fusing interior, architectural and landscape design.

In the 18th and early 19th centuries, colonial gentry brought European design fashion to America, establishing their estates in more agricultural than suburban settings. Live-oak allées and symmetrical parterres of plantations in the South continued French Renaissance landscape design traditions. Tidewater and Carolina estates such as Middleton Place (1755) incorporated the English Renaissance garden style characterized by formality near the house and pastoral, distant lawns and gardens. The *ferme ornées* of Washington's Mount Vernon (1799) and Jefferson's Monticello (1768–1809) represent early adaptations of a transitional era of landscape design. They retained some formal English Renaissance landscape elements, while adapting the romantic principles of 18th-century British landscape gardeners Batty Langley and Humphry Repton to uniquely American landscapes, such as combining rather than isolating formal and informal design elements.

A different estate landscape—and a more suburban setting—evolved in the early 19th century as wealthy industrial barons developed sylvan retreats away from post-

Gould estate (1909, Stephen Child), Santa Barbara, Calif., designed to reflect a regional approach to this landscape surrounded by low foothills. (Elwood, *American Landscape Architecture*, 1924)

Walkway, Marshall Field estate, Lloyds Neck, Long Island, N.Y., showing a rich use of plant materials by Marian Coffin, one of the many women landscape architects who contributed to landscape design. (ASLA, *Illustrations of Work of Members*, 1932)

Industrial Revolution cities. These extensive but seldom-farmed estates first appeared on the outskirts of Boston and in the scenic Hudson River Valley. Here, landscape designers further adapted English landscape school premises to this dramatic regional landscape using the valley's picturesque landscape scenery as an aesthetic. Hyde Park (1828,

André Parmentier), Dutchess County, N.Y., typified these naturalistic landscape designs. Straight lines gave way to more natural shapes, with entrance drives curving toward the house, providing changes of scenery and glimpses of structures or landscape beyond. Andrew Jackson Downing popularized this style of estate design. With associates Calvert Vaux and Alexander J. Davis, he combined the picturesque qualities of the Gothic Revival with the informality of the landscape to form a unified composition. Downing extolled the landscapes at Montgomery Place (1802–63), Dutchess County, N.Y., Blythewood (c. 1835), Annandale-on-Hudson, N.Y., and Wodenthe (1825–41), Beacon, N.Y., as examples of this ideal.

Frederick Law Olmsted extended this American romantic school of landscape design through a more pastoral style reminiscent of New England's rural landscape. Examples include the Phillips estate (1881), Beverly, Mass., with its well-defined landscape spaces bounded by informal plant groupings, and Biltmore (1888–95), Asheville, N.C., the pinnacle of the romantic era in estate design. For Biltmore, Olmsted designed a winding drive through the pastoral and wooded outer landscape, which gave way to elaborate formal gardens surrounding the house. While the larger estate grounds at Biltmore refined the pastoral Olmstedian style, the design for elaborate formal gardens, perhaps influenced by Olmsted's associate Henry Sargent Codman, ushered in a new era of estate design.

Estate landscapes developed from 1880 to 1920 were part of an unparalleled era of economic growth, resulting in unrestrained displays of wealth. Influenced by the Ecole des Beaux Arts, balance, symmetry and spatial hierarchies in architecture were transferred directly to the garden and landscape. Loggias and porches opened to outdoor formal terraces. Central foyers and halls extended to outdoor vistas through formal lawns, parterres or water cascades.

While many estates from 1890 to 1930 were the singular creations of architects such as McKim, Mead and White, Carrère and Hastings, and Delano and Aldrich, collaboration between architects and landscape architects was widespread, marking the increasing acceptance and popularity of landscape architecture as a design art. Charles A. Platt, who was uniquely qualified as both architect and landscape architect, executed many important projects during this elegant era. The work of Ferruccio Vitale, Fletcher Steele, Olmsted Brothers, Warren H. Manning and Jens Jensen highlight early 20th-century estate landscape design. Women practitioners such as Beatrix Jones Farrand, Marian Coffin, Ellen Biddle Shipman and Rose Nichols also played prominent roles.

The Depression brought the estate era of American landscape architecture to a close. In the last several decades many of the great estates have been demolished, their landscapes subdivided. The modern era, however, is not without its own examples of country estates, although these tend to be more modest in scale. The curvilinear informality of the Donnell residence (1948, Thomas Church) in Sonoma, Calif., complements the pastoral scenery of surrounding hills and marshes. Residential landscape designs of A. E. Bye continue the naturalist tradition of estate design, whereas the allées and bosques of places such as the Miller residence (1955, Dan Kiley) in Columbus, Ind., adapt classic French and Beaux Arts garden formality to a contemporary setting. 🖋

McCann estate, Oyster Bay, Long Island, N.Y., by Annette Hoyt Flanders, where trees soften the edges of a formal garden and a pavilion provides a focal point at the end of an axis. (ASLA, 1932)

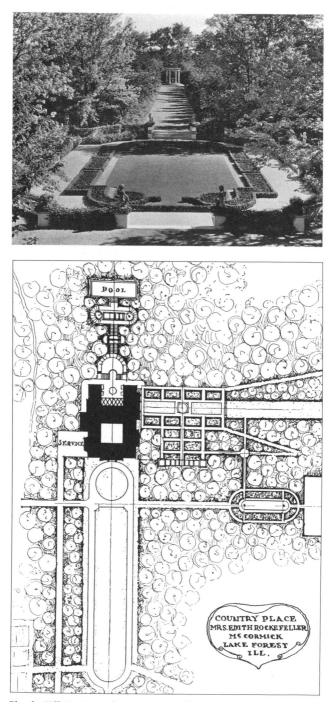

Plan for Villa Turicum, the estate of Harold and Edith Rockefeller McCormick, Lake Forest, Ill., 1912, an expert adaptation by Charles A. Platt of Italian principles to a sloping site. (*Architectural Record*, January 1924)

Otto Kahn estate, Syosset, Long Island, N.Y., c. 1923, designed by
Delano and Aldrich, a highly styled estate influenced by French
Renaissance formality. (Elwood)

Above: Plan for Vizcaya, the estate of James Deering, Miami, 1917, designed by Diego Suarez and Paul Chalfin with special attention to detail and the tropical environment. (Vizcaya)

Center: Whitemarsh Hall (1921, Jacques Greber), the estate of Edward Stotesbury, Chestnut Hill, Pa., designed to reflect the landscape of Versailles. (Library of Congress)

GARDENS
Jory Johnson

Native Americans made horticultural contributions to the early colonial settlements but had little influence on garden design. Until the late 18th century, most Americans could seldom afford time for anything more than utilitarian gardens and flower beds. In the South, plantation owners took advantage of commanding river vistas and slave labor to build expansive mansions and grounds; their central-axis gardens and long allées were influenced by English Renaissance gardens. Later, in the early 19th century, large country estates in the rugged Hudson River topography favored the casual, picturesque style promoted by Andrew Jackson Downing.

In the latter part of the 19th and early 20th centuries, exotic plants and garden ornaments became widely available. Fashionable Victorian embellishments—star-shaped flower beds and banks of the latest cultivars of lilacs, roses and hollyhocks—spread through the new "railroad suburbs" of large cities. Frank Scott and other popular garden writers gave detailed recommendations for foundation plantings (over which there was wide disagreement on the necessity to conceal foundations with billowing shrubery), front yards and other problems confronting suburban homeowners. Special garden features were emphasized such as sentimental fountains or colorful rings of red cannas, spirea, geraniums and other larger, showy flowers. Also popular were informal or wild gardens, which combined the latest horticultural introductions with a romantic love of nature.

The 1893 World's Columbian Exposition, with its Classical Revival architecture, stimulated interest in formal Italian and French gardens. The writer Edith Wharton and architect and landscape designer Charles A. Platt advocated architectonic elements, including pergolas, summerhouses and balustrades, to achieve a progression of well-defined garden rooms. Formality long continued to be a status symbol for many Americans. The Colonial Revival gardens (1928–37, Arthur A. Shurcliff) at Williamsburg, Va., with

Decorative flower bed and dense foundation planting embellishing a 19th-century residence. (Knox Foundation)

Colonial Revival garden (1941, Alden Hopkins) for Williamsburg, Va. Topiary shrubs add a whimsical element to this design based on 18th-century North Carolina gardens. (Colonial Williamsburg Foundation)

Pergola, Old Westbury Gardens (1906), Long Island, N.Y. Victorian gardens often featured rustic pergolas covered with flowering vines and flanked by billowing shrubs or flowers.

Classical Revival garden (1916),
Reynolda House, Winston-Salem,
N.C. Many early 20th-century
gardens featured clear geometrical
spaces and bold garden
architecture.

Greene House, Pasadena, Calif., a
restored 1907 bungalow enhanced
by a Craftsman-inspired garden
and pool. (Regula Campbell)

Blue Stairs (1926) at Naumkeag, Stockbridge, Mass., where Fletcher
Steele's grove of birch trees acts as a counterpoint to the Art Nouveau
stair rails. (© 1983 Alan Ward)

their small-scale borders and parterres, provided a popular model for the reduced expectations following the Depression, particularly in the South and the Mid-Atlantic states.

California gardens from the late 19th to mid-20th centuries sought inspiration from Mediterranean countries. Irving Gill's unelaborated courtyard gardens, with drought-resistant plantings, were derived from Spanish missions. California landscape architects such as Florence Yoch, Edward Huntsman-Trout, Ralph Cornell and Lockwood De-Forest were accomplished plantsmen and women who closely supervised the construction and maintenance of their gardens. Their projects were strongly influenced by formal Italian gardens and usually included elaborate series of formal lawns and architectonic planting designs. The Craftsman-style bungalow, popularized by Greene and Greene, introduced outdoor living with sleeping porches and terraces. Bungalow gardens frequently were influenced by Japanese prototypes.

The first significant influence of 20th-century art and architecture on American gardens can be found in the work of Fletcher Steele, an admirer of French Art Deco garden experiments of the 1920s. But it was not until International Style architecture arrived on the scene that American landscape architects began to reject formulaic classical plans. In the late 1930s, inspired by the ferment and excitement of the new architectural theories, James Rose, Garrett Eckbo and Dan Kiley began exploring appropriate garden forms and ecological strategies for the modern era. Kiley extended the rectilinearity and open plan of modern architecture into the garden. For Rose and Eckbo, the most important concepts were embodied in Eckbo's book *Landscapes for Living* (1950). Many Americans in the post–Korean War building boom believed that elegant gardens were a luxury or indulgence. Eckbo's home landscaping book showed how such quotidian necessities of suburban life as laundry areas, children's sandboxes and barbecue grills could be part of a sophisticated garden design. Homeowners also were encouraged to use industrial products such as poured concrete and other inexpensive materials.

Many of these ideas were first developed in California by Lawrence Halprin, Robert Royston, Douglas Baylis and others. With its year-round temperate climate, California became synonymous with redwood decks, swimming pools and strong paving and ground plane patterns. The "California style" promised low maintenance and relaxed entertaining. In addition, the incorporation of Japanese garden motifs such as picturesque moss beds, evergreens, ferns and artfully placed stones were considered an ideal response to the cool refinement of contemporary-style homes.

By the 1970s various economic and resource pressures reduced the average size of residential lots. In addition, smaller families had less need for all-purpose yards. Many homeowners also were growing tired of large suburban lawns and the blandness of low-maintenance gardens. The environmental movement helped evoke an interest in natural landscapes, including the aesthetic pleasures of perennial gardens, ornamental grasses and garden architecture. Recent garden design has been influenced by the historic

Hamilton Garden (1957), a private design in Indiana by Dan Kiley, who wanted to "create a rich variety of spaces and experiences." (© 1978 Alan Ward)

Opposite: Garrett Eckbo Garden (1959), Los Angeles, where Eckbo's use of aluminum and other modern materials creates a landscape for living. (Julius Shulman)

preservation movement, which has increased public awareness of America's garden history. It is doubtful, however, that Americans will return *en masse* to historical revival styles.

The history of the garden in America could be described as a movement from revivals or copies of European styles to an exploration of America's social, cultural and geographical diversity. While American gardens have not achieved a singular style, the latter half of the 20th century represents the first consistent break with classical ideals and European models. As new styles and directions are developed, and as American gardens begin to receive the same attention now given to European and Asian gardens, their rich heritage will achieve deserved recognition. 🖋

Soros Garden (1967, A. E. Bye and Peter Johnson), Southhampton, N.Y., where careful grading and planting create a pattern of melting snow and shadows. (A. E. Bye)

HISTORIC LANDSCAPES
Suzanne Louise Turner

Landscape architecture in America has a relatively short history when compared to that of Europe or Asia, yet Americans have become increasingly aware of the need to preserve significant landscapes so that future generations can understand their predecessors' relationship to the land. But, whereas the preservation of buildings is a straightforward process of protecting or restoring architectural fabric, the preservation of landscapes composed of organic tissue and subject to the vagaries of climate and natural processes is a far more complicated undertaking.

Some of the first landscapes and gardens to be recognized as worthy of preservation were sites associated with important persons such as George Washington's Mount Vernon (1799) and Thomas Jefferson's Monticello (1768–1809) and outstanding gardens such as those at Middleton Place (1755).

The Williamsburg restoration, initiated in 1926, marked a new era in preservation by focusing not simply on isolated buildings, but on the historic environment as a whole. The gardens of the Governor's Palace and the aristocracy were depicted alongside utilitarian landscapes—kitchen gardens, pastures and streetscapes. New techniques for researching garden history were also used there, including archeology to locate early land use patterns such as garden layouts and structures.

Another important step in the development of a landscape preservation ethic was the rise of historic districts in the 1930s. The recognition of the importance of entire neighborhoods, beginning with Charleston, S.C., in 1931 and the Vieux Carré in New Orleans in 1937, acknowledged the urban landscape as the glue that binds together fragments of the historic environment. This new commit-

Opposite: Kitchen garden, Williamsburg, Va. (Colonial Williamsburg Foundation)

Kitchen garden, Monticello, Charlottesville, Va. (Peter Hatch, Monticello)

ment to protect the *tout ensemble*—the sum of the buildings and open spaces, rather than just individual structures—also moved preservation from a museum mentality, in which each element is frozen in time, to a concern for dynamic, livable neighborhoods and, ultimately, for the rural landscape as well.

Since the Bicentennial in 1976 and the popularization of preservation, the definition of significant landscapes has been broadened beyond high-style gardens to encompass urban parks, such as those designed by Frederick Law Olmsted and his associates; vernacular or common landscapes, such as agricultural districts and distinctive ethnic settlements; and industrial enclaves, such as the mining regions of Pennsylvania and the manufacturing town of Lowell, Mass. Landscapes are now considered important on their own merits, rather than principally in association with a famous person or building.

Today, highly refined technologies, such as remote sensing and pollen identification, have been used to help piece together the story and appearance of landscapes that have disappeared or decayed. For those that remain, federal agencies are making major contributions to protect and document significant landscapes: guidelines have been written for nominating landscapes to the National Register of Historic Places, and both the Historic American Buildings Survey and the Historic American Engineering Record are committed to documenting landscapes. The National Park Service has studied rural landscapes under its jurisdiction and has established policies for their protection, including nominating them to the National Register as rural districts. Legislation has been introduced in Congress to provide for the inventory, documentation and protection of the work of the Olmsted firm, activities supported by a private coalition, the National Association for Olmsted Parks. Archives are being established to collect records of designed landscapes in many states and regions. A national clearinghouse, the Catalog of Landscape Records in the United States, was established in 1987 by Wave Hill in New York City, with support from the National Endowment for the Arts.

Interest in landscape history has never been higher. But the challenge for the future goes beyond documenting and protecting sites and ensuring their survival. It calls for creative interpretation that will communicate to the public not only what landscapes of the past looked like, but, more important, the meaning of these places in the lives of people who shaped them. 🍃

The Battery, Charleston, S.C. As the first local historic district in the United States, Charleston served as a model for protecting the integrity of vital urban neighborhoods. (Jane Iseley)

Above: Agricultural land near Amana, Iowa, an important component of rural America now threatened by the pressures of suburbanization and agribusiness. (Amana Heritage Society)

Center: Ashley River Road, near Charleston, S.C., where trees are protected by a Dorchester County ordinance that limits tree removal. Areas of the road in a neighboring county are not protected.

God's Acre, Old Salem, N.C., part of the distinctive landscape created by the Moravians when they settled here in 1766. (Suzanne Turner)

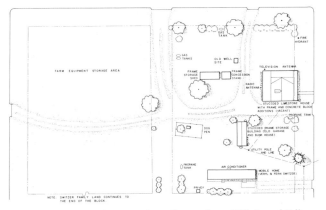

Above: Black settler's homestead, Nicodemus, Kans., part of a 1983 Historic American Buildings Survey project marking a broadening of its work to encompass both vernacular and designed landscapes. (HABS)

Center: Sugar Mill, Laurel Valley Plantation, Thibodaux, La., an agricultural and industrial landscape representing a continuity of land use for two centuries. (Suzanne Turner)

HOUSING ENVIRONMENTS
Michael Laurie

The house represents shelter, privacy and security for a family or group, and a cluster of houses—of families—constitutes a community. The quality of our communities and thus the lifestyles they support is a function of many factors, including provision for streets, spacing of dwellings, availability of private gardens, distribution of public open space and relationship to the work place. Site planning for housing is a major contribution of the modern landscape architect.

Historically, the Jeffersonian dream of single-family farms equidistantly spaced in an agricultural landscape and William Penn's compact plan for Philadelphia (1683) were two contrasting alternatives for community form in 18th-century America. Later, the desire to get away from the squalor and congestion of industrialized 19th-century cities resulted in the development of suburbs. Connected by trolley and railroad services, suburban communities combined the pleasures of the countryside with the economic and cultural opportunities of the city. H. W. S. Cleveland, Frederick Law Olmsted and other pioneer landscape architects designed such suburbs with winding, tree-planted streets, single-family homes and surrounding lawns. Natural features were emphasized, and public greens and small parks provided a romantic landscape setting for the villas. A good example of the romantic suburb is Riverside, Ill. (1868–70), near Chicago, designed by Olmsted and Vaux.

Although this housing type was largely for the middle class and, therefore, not widely affordable, it did provide a model for those concerned with a general improvement in housing conditions. The garden city ideal, defined in England by Ebenezer Howard in 1898, resulted in complete towns of limited size for lower-income families such as Letchworth (1908) and Wellwyn (1924).

Inspired by these examples, the socially conscious architects Clarence Stein and Henry Wright designed Radburn, N.J. (1928–29). There, a new factor, the automobile, was incorporated into the design. A system of 40-acre superblocks with cul-de-sac access to the houses retained a central green space with pedestrian paths from every street at grade. Six superblocks made up a neighborhood with approximately 960 dwellings at an overall density of four per acre.

At Baldwin Hills (1941), Los Angeles, the same architects, with landscape architect Fred Barlow, further developed this model for rental units. One large superblock of 80 acres accommodated 627 units, with parking provided at a ratio of three to one. Private patios opened onto pedestrian ways giving access to a central village green, one-half mile long and varying from 50 to 250 feet in width.

In spite of the apparent advantages of these communities, America's private-sector housing built after World War II was dominated by the subdivision concept epitomized by Levittown, N.J. (1955). Exceptions occurred in the public and corporate sectors, where, following European practice, often massive housing blocks were surrounded by green space and playgrounds. Stuyvesant Town (1947) in New York City is a notable example. In other situations, such as the new towns of Irvine, Calif. (1964), Reston, Va. (1964), and Columbia, Md. (1965), a variety of housing types from highrise apartments and cluster housing to conventional

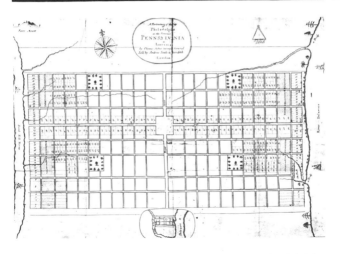

William Penn's plan for Philadelphia.

Left and below: Schematic plan for a Radburn, N.J., superblock and a typical Radburn sidewalk, with front yards leading to a shared walkway. (Newark Public Library)

subdivisions were combined into planned environments, including spacious and accessible green areas for recreation while achieving an economical overall density.

In the future the planned unit, condominium and rental development and the typical subdivision with single-family homes are likely to undergo change as new concerns—social cohesion, affordable housing, resource conservation, water quality, solar orientation and travel time to work—are taken seriously. The Village Homes development (1972) of Michael Corbett in Davis, Calif., with solar orientation for all houses, narrow streets, bicycle and pedestrian paths, community gardens and facilities, and drought-tolerant planting is a recent example responding to many of these issues. 🖋

Park, Riverside, Ill., where Olmsted and Vaux created a fully integrated setting for housing and recreational pursuits.

Plan for federal public housing, Taft, Calif., 1941, with landscape planning by Garrett Eckbo. (Eckbo, *Landscape for Living*, 1980)

Levittown, N.Y. (1947), an example of the more typical suburban development after World War II in which a public green space was sacrificed to provide for more housing units. (Levittown Public Library)

Village Homes (1972, Michael Corbett), Davis, Calif., marking a return
to more community-based activities and concerns.

Plan for Village Homes in Davis, showing the use of green areas and how
residences are grouped into neighborhoods.

INSTITUTIONAL AND CORPORATE LANDSCAPES
Cheryl Barton

In its concern with providing meaningful open space, landscape architecture has always related fundamentally to human welfare. Institutional environments have benefited from the expertise of landscape architects for more than a century, but the corporate landscape is a more recent phenomenon. In the 18th and early 19th centuries, institutions existed primarily to take care of problems that the family was unable to handle—care of the mentally retarded, orphaned children, the sick and the handicapped. Many of these places were little more than warehouses. A similar fate met workers during the Industrial Revolution who fled their farms to grasp opportunities in the cities. There, too, they were confined in warehouse-type environments for long, exhausting hours.

Reflecting post–Civil War reform movements, American landscape architects demonstrated innovative and practical responses to the social problems of alcoholism, mental illness and disease in the design of new institutional settings. Pure air and water, sunlight and other natural amenities were important factors in planning hospitals, asylums and sanatoriums. Spacious, well-designed grounds reflected advances in medicine. These projects could involve many disciplines and were often coordinated by landscape architects whose knowledge of environmental factors provided the requisite overview.

Frederick Law Olmsted, once secretary of the U.S. Sanitary Commission (later the American Red Cross), planned several significant institutions, including the Columbia Institution for the Deaf (1866) in Washington, D.C. The plan for the Iowa Hospital for the Insane (1871, H. W. S. Cleveland), Mt. Pleasant, involved patients in the therapeutic planting of native trees and shrubs on the asylum grounds. Scientific evidence has indicated that direct contact with nature produces positive effects on healing. Today, site and building design for contemporary institutions place a premium on exterior views for patients as well as easy accessibility to courtyards and gardens.

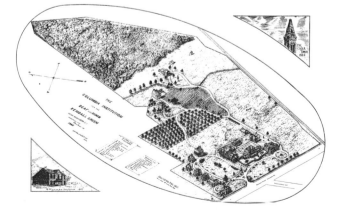

Columbia Institution, now Gallaudet University, Washington, D.C., 1885, designed to give residents the benefits of a rural setting. (Gallaudet University Archives)

Opposite: Iowa Hospital for the Insane, Mt. Pleasant, Iowa, the oldest mental hospital west of the Mississippi. (Mount Pleasant Treatment Center)

The corporate landscape evolved after World War II because of rapid growth in industry and the advent of suburbia. Here, the symbolism of wealth and power was expressed in attractive, parklike locations. People now spend considerable time in corporate settings, which in many places have replaced Main Street as a community's social crossroads. Affinities with early country villas and manor houses have also been suggested, as these buildings and their elaborate grounds once housed a large population of family and servants, curiously analogous to 20th-century managerial, clerical and maintenance staff.

Today's corporate headquarters landscapes, such as those for Deere and Company (1963, Sasaki Associates), Moline, Ill., an important precedent; Carlson Center (1988, EDAW Design Group), Minnetonka, Minn.; and Pacific Bell (1987, MPA Design), San Ramon, Calif., contain extensive open space and recreational resources for their work forces, including tennis and volleyball courts, jogging paths, sculpture gardens, lakes and other facilities to ensure more loyal and productive workers and to add value to the corporate real estate portfolio. Furthermore, such features convey image, status, power, prestige and product excellence— critical ingredients in a competitive corporate culture.

For many suburbs, the corporation has become a community center. In its commitment to employees and the public, PepsiCo (1965, Edward D. Stone, Jr., Associates)— an integration of landscape architecture, architecture and sculpture in Purchase, N.Y.—exemplified a new creativity in the corporate landscape of its time. Its sculpture collection is displayed in garden terraces, becoming an outdoor art museum for the public and a showpiece landscape for the corporate landlord. Many corporations have purchased former estates and preserved their historic landscapes. At Corporate Woods (1976, The SWA Group), Overland Park, Kans., and the TRW World Headquarters (1985, Sasaki Associates), Lyndhurst, Ohio, landscape architects have effectively contrasted contemporary architecture with wooded and pastoral settings. Codex's world headquarters (1986, Hanna/Olin), Canton, Mass., incorporates an elegant interior atrium at the heart of its complex of buildings to recall the outdoors year-round.

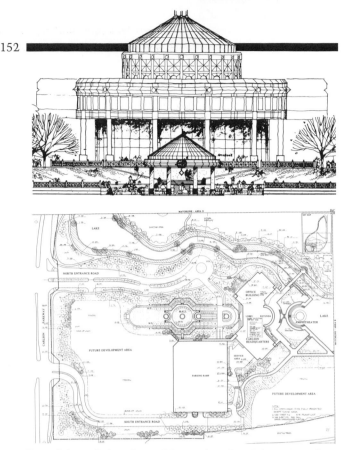

Top and above: Carlson Center, Minnetonka, Minn. A dramatic outdoor performance area and theater provide special amenities for staff and the public. (EDAW Design Group)

Urban corporate landscapes, which were the earliest examples, also have thrived. One innovation was the Kaiser roof garden (1960, Osmundson and Staley), Oakland, Calif., a three-acre urban open space 23 stories above the street. While 90 percent of the site is covered by the building, 60 percent actually becomes semipublic open space. Dallas's Fountain Place (1985, Dan Kiley), with a similar open space ratio, is a shimmering, monumental water garden in sharp contrast to the arid Texas landscape.

Increasingly, site plans have been developed to express particular corporate and institutional values. The Christian Science Church's world headquarters (1973, Sasaki Associates) in Boston is a powerful, ceremonial space, personifying the church's social stature and wealth. Landscape architects and their clients have approached corporate site design as an art form, creating dramatic tension between geometric and biomorphic forms. Rich materials and sculpture abound in Williams Square (1984, The SWA Group), Las Colinas, Tex., where regional land forms are borrowed and reinterpreted on the site. In Englewood, Colo., the mission of Chevron Geothermal (1985, Hargreaves Associates) is depicted metaphorically by its landscape of exfoliating layers of sedimentary rock and simulated steam. The desired effect is a more memorable and enduring image.

The significance of the institutional and corporate landscape types today is that they have demonstrated that both quality open space and memorable imagery are vital to the human experience. 🏶

Opposite: Codex World Headquarters, Canton, Mass., featuring a 14,000-square-foot atrium garden. The 11-acre corporate campus lies on a restored horse farm. (Steve Rosenthal)

Deere and Company Administrative Center, Moline, Ill., designed to enhance the natural beauty of the rural site. (Randy Horine)

TRW World Headquarters, Lyndhurst, Ohio, a contemporary office in a pastoral setting. (© 1985 Alan Ward)

Kaiser Center Roof Garden, Oakland, Calif., which advanced construction techniques for roof gardens throughout the world. (Theodore Osmundson)

Fountain Place, Dallas, an engaging water garden at the base of the Allied Bank Tower. (James F. Wilson)

William Square, Las Colinas, Tex., where the plaza design sets off a sculpture by Robert Glen. (Tom Fox, The SWA Group)

Christian Science Center, Boston, world headquarters for the First
Church of Christ, Scientist, which includes nine acres of open space.
(Hutchins Photography)

Computerized map of Hadley, Mass., assessing the significance of farmland for land use planning. Recent advances in computer technology have made such assessments affordable at the local level. Shaded areas indicate most significant (horizontal rules), highly significant (grid), significant (black) and other agricultural (diagonal rules) lands. (METLAND Landscape Planning Research Group, University of Massachusetts)

Pine Run (1965), Camden, N.J. The development protects large wooded areas for recreation and open space, minimizes erosion and collects water runoff into a lake on the site. (John Rahenkamp Consulting)

LANDSCAPE PLANNING
Julius Gy. Fabos

The entire American population depends daily on our national landscape for work, for food and industrial production and for recreation. More than three million acres of land are converted from rural to urban use in the United States each year. We build about one and a half million homes and various commercial, industrial, institutional and recreational facilities annually. We dispose of millions of tons of waste into the air, water and soil and crisscross the country with roads, railroads, transmission lines and pipelines. With all these activities, we as a nation deeply affect the quality and value of the environment we occupy.

The rich bounties of this country as well as its varied and ample landscape can provide us with a sound and beautiful environment—but only if we extensively apply landscape planning principles. Landscape planning takes place in many ways. Currently, the most widely used application occurs within the realm of project site planning. Increasingly, more developers around the country are employing the services of landscape architects in such endeavors. The results are more attractive, are more environmentally suitable and make more economic sense than those without such planning expertise.

Frederick Law Olmsted, the father of American landscape architecture, was absorbed in all aspects of landscape planning. He was most instrumental in initiating the successful national park movement. He planned the first model community, preserving the riverfront for public open space in Riverside, Ill. (1868–70). He also linked three communities in Boston by transforming the Muddy River into a spectacular linear park in the 1880s. His pupils Charles Eliot and Eliot's nephew, Charles Eliot II, expanded Olmsted's vision into a statewide open space plan for Massachusetts. This visionary concept is still being implemented.

After World War II the Olmstedian tradition was continued at every level. Ian McHarg emerged as the most important voice of landscape planning during the 1960s. His seminal book, *Design with Nature* (1969), established contemporary principles of landscape planning ranging from shaping development in response to natural values to preserving critical landscape resources. Another leader of landscape planning at this time was Philip H. Lewis, Jr., who initiated a creative statewide recreation plan in Wisconsin that established environmental corridors throughout the state. The environmental movement provided landscape planners with many opportunities during the turbulent decade of the 1960s. They were called on to make critical land use decisions and assess the visual and cultural features of large regions. They developed sophisticated procedures to assess diverse landscape qualities. And they helped determine the amount and type of development for urbanizing regions.

Since the 1970s landscape planners have worked increasingly with scientists to obtain relevant findings about the impact of humans on the landscape. Thus, planning has become even more complex. Landscape planning research groups have sprung up to develop procedures capable of synthesizing scientific knowledge to provide a foundation for more intelligent land use decisions.

Current landscape planning is responding to the ever-

Open space plan for Massachusetts, still in use today, a product of the Open Space Commission appointed by the governor in 1928 to deal with the state's recreational needs. (Fabos, *Land Use Planning*, 1985)

Plan for the Valleys (1963, Ian McHarg) for Baltimore County, Md., showing how the landscape architect related the level of development density to the degree of forest cover in forested and unforested plateaus and a forested valley. (McHarg, *Design with Nature*, 1969)

increasing amount of new scientific information and has turned to computers for help. Jack Dangermond, through his firm, ESRI, the current leader in this trend toward computerization, has developed the most advanced geographic information systems to deal with the myriad of spatial data now essential for determining land use policies at all levels. Other leading landscape planners, including Laura Muessig and Allen Robinette, are using these procedures in forecasting and managing land use changes in the state of Minnesota. Current research has also been exploring the utility of computer technology for landscape planning at the community level. We will soon see these emerging procedures used in many types of site planning.

Landscape planning has a bright and challenging future. Planning the landscape has become the most significant of all land use objectives. In the information age, landscape planning can help us use our resources more intelligently than we ever have before. ✍

Wisconsin Heritage Trails proposal (1964, Phil Lewis). The most significant areas are identified by the smallest dot pattern; blank areas are least significant. The analysis was made by examining the concentration of 220 natural and cultural resources in the state. (*Landscape Architecture*, January 1964)

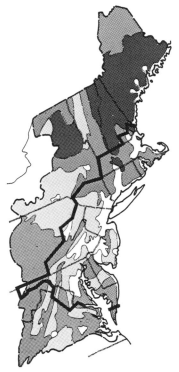

Visual and cultural values of the North Atlantic region in 1970. The degree of landscape quality is indicated by the shaded areas. (Research Planning and Design Associates)

Below: 1987 analysis of the impact of acid rain in Minnesota, an example of computer-aided land use planning. (Land Management Information Center)

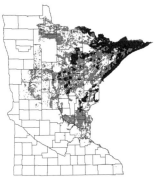

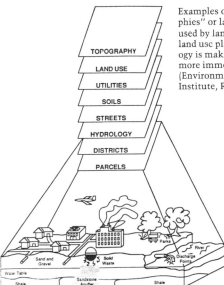

Examples of some of the "geographies" or layers of information used by landscape architects in land use planning. New technology is making this type of analysis more immediate and accurate. (Environmental Systems Research Institute, Redlands, Calif.)

LANDSCAPE SCENERY
Wayne G. Tlusty

Landscape scenery has become a highly valued resource. For well over a century, major changes in attitudes toward scenic landscapes have generally paralleled the development of landscape architecture as a profession. Recognizing the innate qualities of pastoral beauty, Andrew Jackson Downing influenced American sensitivity to landscape appreciation. His landscapes illustrated how gardens could be linked visually to the countryside. Downing also was an early advocate for bringing natural beauty to urban areas through public parks. Frederick Law Olmsted and Calvert Vaux designed most of Central Park as idealized natural scenery, emulating the best examples of meadows, forests, hills, lakes and streams. Their approach to creating parks was widely followed throughout America and fostered a new awareness of landscape scenery.

During the mid-19th century, writers, painters and naturalists began discovering and focusing on spectacular American landscapes in the Hudson River Valley and the West. Their work in the West led to federal recognition of the need to preserve natural scenery for all citizens. In 1865 Frederick Law Olmsted developed a management philosophy for Yosemite, addressing both preservation and public use in the world's first scenic landscape reserved for public enjoyment. Olmsted's philosophy for the preserve served as a model for our present national park system.

Broadening the concept from public to private lands, landscape architect Frank Waugh sought recognition also for scenic beauty in the countryside, advocating that all citizens had an inalienable right to enjoy fine rural scenery. In his 1910 book he wrote about the need to maintain pastoral, utilitarian scenery and the inherent beauty of agricultural landscapes. Waugh maintained that "beauty does not interfere with utility, nor utility with beauty—the two are sisters."

Yosemite Valley, Calif., the first scenic area preserved by the federal government. (Wayne Tlusty)

Opposite: Trappers Lake, Colo., site of the first application of the wilderness concept. (Wayne Tlusty)

Badlands National Park, S.D., an eroded sculptured landscape providing dramatic scenery without the presence of mountains, water or vegetation. (Wayne Tlusty)

Managed forest setting in Wisconsin, typical of millions of acres of public and private lands providing a recreational setting for hundreds of thousands of visitors each year. (Wayne Tlusty)

Upper Missouri River in Montana, one of several waterways whose scenic beauty is protected under the 1968 National Wild and Scenic Rivers Act. (Wayne Tlusty)

The first applied wilderness policy evolved from efforts to protect Trappers Lake in Colorado. As the landscape architect for the U.S. Forest Service, Arthur H. Carhart was directed in 1919 to provide recommendations for seasonal homes along the undeveloped shoreline. His proposal—that the area's scenic beauty should remain pristine and permanently free of development for all generations—was adopted.

Scenic preservation received a boost in 1954, when the U.S. Supreme Court (in *Berman* v. *Parker*) recognized that aesthetics alone was a sufficient reason to regulate land development. The environmental movement of the 1960s brought about more public awareness of landscape scenery in America. The National Conference on Natural Beauty in 1965 placed landscape scenery on the nation's environmental agenda. During this period many landscape architects made significant contributions to protecting and enhancing the aesthetic quality of America's landscape. The Wisconsin studies by Philip Lewis in the early 1960s established a process to identify environmental corridors that included areas of notable scenery. A 1964 study for Sea Ranch in California by Lawrence Halprin was a model for protecting open space and scenery while allowing planned development. Ian McHarg used ecological determinants to structure land use planning and protect visual character.

In 1969 the National Environmental Policy Act stressed the "continuing responsibility" of the federal government to ensure aesthetically and culturally pleasing surroundings. It required the development of methods to measure

how landscape contributes to the quality of life. As one example, Forest Service landscape architects in 1974 developed a visual resource management process, which was applied to 190 million acres of public land. Other approaches were designed to address visual resource needs for roads, shorelines, agricultural areas, utility corridors and development in the urban fringe. Since 1964 the Interior Department has designated a number of natural areas deemed to be of national significance as Registered Natural Landmarks.

Today, regard for landscape scenery has evolved into a broad recognition of the landscape as a vital national resource. In many areas, well-established policies now guide economic development to preserve scenic character, mitigate adverse intrusions and establish desired visual qualities. Landscape architects have provided critical leadership in protecting landscape scenery. 🖋

Top: Wisconsin farmland. The visually dramatic contours follow good conservation practices. (B-Wolfgang Hoffmann, University of Wisconsin)

Opposite and left: Graphic simulation used to manage visual change of rural landscapes in Massachusetts—the site before development, after typical development and with creative development. (Center for Rural Massachusetts, University of Massachusetts)

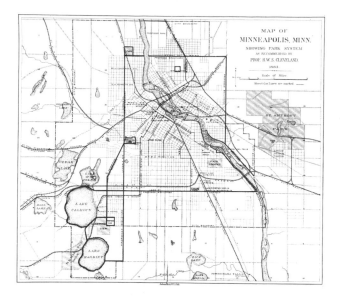

Proposal for a system of parks and parkways for Minneapolis by H.W. S. Cleveland, 1883.

Right and below: West River Parkway and West Minnehaha Parkway, Minneapolis. A recreational roadway and pedestrian trails explore woodland settings within the city.

METROPOLITAN OPEN SPACES
Roger B. Martin

As with many aspects of landscape architecture, precedents for metropolitan park systems can be traced to Europe. In early 19th-century Germany, for example, Prince Pückler-Muskau, a benevolent aristocrat, converted his ancestral lands in Silesia into an extensive parklike system. His desire was to surround the town of Muskau "in such a way that it would become merely part of the park." As American cities expanded, several early landscape architects, inspired by the work of Pückler-Muskau and others, envisioned vast open space systems extending through and around the nation's growing urban regions.

Linear parks, or parkways, connecting significant parkland within a metropolitan area were pioneered by Frederick Law Olmsted, Calvert Vaux and H. W. S. Cleveland. The latter in 1869 recommended a 14-mile "grand avenue," similar to the tree-lined boulevards of Europe, connecting Chicago's parks. An early project by Olmsted and Vaux—Brooklyn's Eastern Parkway (1870) and another by Olmsted and his firm, Arborway, part of Boston's urban park system (1878–95)—incorporated this feature. To accommodate American needs, however, the two landscape architects provided a generous strip of land for carriages, equestrian trails and pedestrian walks.

As early as 1872, H. W. S. Cleveland advocated a bold metropolitan park system for the growing cities of Minneapolis and St. Paul. Included would be the nearby Mississippi River bluffs and land encompassing the region's picturesque lakes, hills and valleys, plus additional small inner-city parks. He also proposed radial avenues and tree-lined boulevards plunging deep into the central city.

In 1890 Charles Eliot suggested a metropolitan system of open spaces for greater Boston. The following year, Massachusetts established the Trustees of Public Reservations to acquire and hold land for public use. As this organization's secretary and later its consulting landscape architect, Eliot worked to establish a Metropolitan Park Commission and formulated an elaborate park plan. His park system included ocean frontage, islands in the inner bay, tidal estuaries, wild forest areas and numerous small squares, playgrounds and parks; boulevards and parkways were added in 1894 as connecting links. While unique to Boston's geography, the plan established the framework for other metropolitan open space networks in America.

A system of parkways with sizable areas for recreation was achieved on a regional scale in Westchester County, N.Y., during the early 20th century. This second-generation metropolitan park system used a parkland corridor to link major park facilities and provide a continuous recreational experience. The financial success of the automobile parkway along the Bronx River resulted in legislation establishing the Westchester County Park Commission in 1922. As a result of his accomplishments on the Bronx River Parkway during the second decade of this century, Gilmore D. Clarke was appointed landscape architect for the county, and he skillfully coordinated planning for thousands of acres of parks and parkways. The linear park system connected large recreational facilities incorporating

Opposite: Temescal Regional Park, East Bay Regional Park District, Oakland, Calif. A designed landscape provides a dramatic setting for a swimming area created from an existing water reservoir.

Westchester County Park System, N.Y., linking a number of parks in the 1920s through a system of scenic parkways.

Opposite: Lake County Forest Preserve District, Ill., where abandoned farmlands have been put to use for a number of recreational pursuits along a 35-mile river corridor.

golf, swimming, amusements, hiking and other activities.

The evolution of metropolitan park systems during the mid-20th century saw continuing emphasis on providing active recreation in a natural setting. Hundreds of miles of hiking trails within large suburban park reserves throughout the United States provided opportunities for exploring nature in close proximity to home and work. Northern California's East Bay Regional Park District illustrates further refinement of the metropolitan open space system concept. During the 1960s, under the direction of landscape architect William Penn Mott (later director of the National Park Service), the system grew to more than 70,000 acres of diversified parkland with more than 1,000 miles of trails. Included were lands that protected unique components such as geological formations and vegetation of interest to science, as well as natural and cultural features, and provided a wide range of recreational opportunities for the 1,500-square-mile area's growing population.

In the future, landscape architects will continue to bring their vision, creativity and understanding of the landscape to the metropolitan open space needs of America's growing urban population. Current metropolitan park systems in rapidly expanding urban areas are exploring new and creative ways to find and permanently protect regional open space. In the Chicago area, vital regional facilities will be provided well into the 21st century through the Open Lands Project, a nonprofit agency working with the Lake County Forest Preserve District, under the direction of landscape architect Jerry Soesbe. More than 12,000 acres of open land have been preserved through private funding since the project was initiated in 1963. More of this type of protection will be needed to ensure a balance in our urban settings between development and open space. 🌿

Opposite: Elm Creek Park Reserve, north of Minneapolis, where this swimming facility evolved from a pond covered with vegetation. The pond was excavated and the bottom fitted with a liner. Several inches of sand were spread over the liner, and water was introduced from a well through a percolation system. (Don King)

Martinez Regional Shoreline, East Bay Regional Park District, Oakland, Calif., combining urban recreation with shoreline wildlife preservation.

NATIONAL FORESTS
Wayne D. Iverson

Although a federal Division of Forestry was established in 1886, it was not until 1891 that forest reserves were actually set aside. In 1905 they were transferred to the U.S. Department of Agriculture's new Forest Service under Gifford Pinchot's leadership and renamed collectively the national forests. These lands, incorporating national forests such as the San Gabriel Forest Reserve near Los Angeles and the Yellowstone Forest Reserve in Wyoming, both among the first set aside, now provide timber, water, wildlife, range and recreation for millions of people.

In 1917, after the Forest Service lost administration of Grand Canyon and other treasured lands to the newly established National Park Service (an action that has spurred rivalry between the two agencies ever since), Frank Waugh was retained as a landscape architectural consultant. Waugh strongly advocated the employment of "landscape engineers" to prepare plans for recreational areas such as campgrounds, picnic areas and even resorts to increase public use of the national forests, which, previously, had been limited to timber harvesting, grazing and water and power production. Arthur Carhart was hired by the Rocky Mountain regional office in 1919 as the first landscape architect for the Forest Service. He initiated forest recreation plans and pioneered wilderness area concepts, but, finding the Forest Service too slow to incorporate ideas, Carhart resigned in 1922.

With the advent of public works programs in the early 1930s, the Forest Service sought to improve its design skills, and in 1934 the agency began hiring landscape architects to design recreational sites and ranger stations for the national forests. Numerous examples of these sturdy rustic-style developments still exist.

Among the 1934 recruits was R. D'Arcy Bonnet, a Harvard graduate who rose within two years from a position with the Monongehela National Forest in West Virginia to one at headquarters in Washington, D.C. Bonnet accompanied consultant Albert Davis Taylor on his second inspection tour of the national forests in 1936. With a decrease in programs, Bonnet was reassigned to the California region in 1939, where he became recognized as the dean of Forest Service landscape architects after more than 30 years' service.

In 1958 Operation Outdoors, a major five-year program to rehabilitate recreational sites, became a significant turning point for landscape architecture in the national forests. For the next two decades the number of landscape architects concentrating on developing the forests' recreational areas steadily increased to a peak of nearly 300 in 1980. In the 1960s several moved into recreation staff positions. By the 1970s some had assumed responsibilities as district rangers and land management planners, and by the 1980s two advanced to forest supervisor positions.

Influential in this expansion and integration of landscape architects was Edward H. Stone II, who became chief landscape architect in 1965. Spurred by the environmental movement and controversies over clear-cutting forests, and with support from top management, he launched an innovative visual resource management program, including training, land management and monitoring functions. The program became a model for other federal agencies. The re-

Arthur Carhart, the first Forest Service landscape architect, on a trip in the Quietco-Superior area of Minnesota, 1920. (Forest Service, USDA)

Ranger station improvement plan (1930s, Forrest H. Jennings), Mark Twain National Forest, Mo. (Forest Service, USDA)

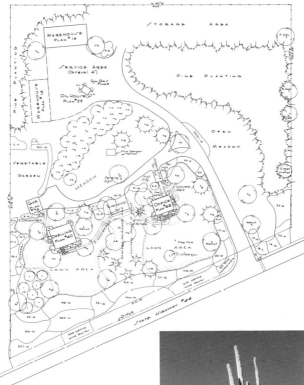

Hikers on a trail in Coronado National Forest, Tucson. (Forest Service, USDA)

Top and above: Log shelters in the 1920s and campfire cooking on national forest lands in the 1930s. (Forest Service, USDA)

search of R. Burton Litton, professor of landscape architecture at the University of California, Berkeley, played an important role in this new program, which maintained a set of performance standards set up by Forest Service landscape architect Warren Bacon and others to manage scenic quality and to protect natural resources. For instance, standards guiding the harvesting of trees dictated the size and shape of the area to be cut. The system became a cornerstone in developing other visual resource management systems in the United States and abroad and was the basis for a popular series of Forest Service handbooks. Another major advance brought about by the Forest Service was the development of sophisticated computer applications for "seen area" mapping and computer perspectives to determine visual impacts.

Landscape architecture in the Forest Service has evolved from a few young men engaged primarily in site planning to several hundred men and women actively involved in managing all the resources of 185 million acres of prime American landscape. Today, no new forest lands are being added to the national stock, but where once national forests were broken up to make management easier, some now are being combined to make management more efficient. 🌿

Playground in a national forest, early 1930s. (Forest Service, USDA)

Hiking bridge in a southeastern national forest, designed by a Forest Service landscape architect. (Forest Service, USDA)

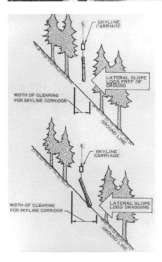

Diagram guiding timber harvesting plans to lessen negative visual impact. (Forest Service, USDA)

Above right and right: Drawing by a landscape architect of a water fountain and the final product, designed to fit into a natural setting. (Forest Service, USDA)

NATIONAL PARKS
Raymond L. Freeman

The world's first national park was established in 1872
when Congress designated more than two million acres in
Wyoming as Yellowstone National Park. By the 1980s
more than 300 diverse parks had been incorporated into
America's world-renowned national park system. The concept of such reserves, pioneered in this country, was a significant contribution to world civilization, and other na-
tions eventually followed this inspiring model.

The history of our national parks and the profession of
landscape architecture have long been intertwined. Today,
about 200 landscape architects have a vital role in providing stewardship for many of our nation's most cherished
natural and cultural resources through the National Park
Service, a part of the U.S. Department of the Interior.

In 1864 President Abraham Lincoln signed legislation
setting aside the magnificent Yosemite Valley and Mariposa Big Tree Groves to be held by the state of California
for "public use, resort and recreation inalienable for all
time." Frederick Law Olmsted was appointed a commis-
sioner for these reservations and supervised the preparation
of an influential report for their administration. In addition
to his skillful plan for managing this park, he advocated a
policy of establishing national parks across the nation and
laid the foundation for our current national park system.

To fill the need for a separate division to oversee these
parks, the secretary of the interior in 1910 recommended
creating a Bureau of National Parks and Resorts specifically
to employ landscape architects for their expertise in planning park development. Three years later the new position
of general superintendent of the national parks was created. Mark Daniels, a practicing landscape architect from
California, filled this job for two years. His most significant accomplishment was bringing sensitive design into
park administration and planning.

It was not until 1916, however, that the National Park
Service was formally established. That year the annual
meeting of the American Society of Landscape Architects
had passed a resolution supporting the National Park Service bill. The ASLA also addressed park issues requiring
landscape architectural expertise, including the delineation
of boundaries in consonance with topography and landscape units and the development of comprehensive plans
for managing natural and developed areas.

Stephen Mather, the first National Park Service director,
took the ASLA recommendations to heart. He and subsequent directors, relying heavily on landscape architects in
guiding the development of the national park system, together with an array of consultants including Frederick
Law Olmsted, Jr., James Pray, Warren H. Manning, Harold
Caparn and James Greenleaf (all former ASLA presidents),
continued the accelerated work of establishing boundaries,
campgrounds, buildings, roadways, bridges and other park
facilities. During this period, a National Park Service landscape architect, Daniel P. Hull, developed a distinctive
nonintrusive, rustic park building design, sometimes referred to as "parkitecture." Built in the early 1920s, the
Ranger Club House, designed by staff landscape architect
Charles P. Punchard, Jr., for the Yosemite National Park in
California, and Hull's Administration Building, now a museum in the Sequoia National Park in California, became

The Ahwahnee (1927), "parkitecture" at Yosemite National Park, Calif. (Carleton Knight III, NTHP)

Hikers at Yosemite. (Richard Frear, National Park Service)

Landscape architects James Greenleaf and Daniel Hull, Washington Lewis, park superintendent, and Arno Camerer, NPS assistant director, studying Yosemite's plan in 1922. (National Park Service)

important symbols of this look for park buildings.

By 1922 the landscape architecture division of the National Park Service, originally located at Yosemite, was moved to San Francisco with Thomas Vint as its influential director. Under Vint the task of creating master plans for each park began in earnest, often with staff landscape architects taking the lead.

During the Depression, many landscape architects were employed temporarily to carry out Civilian Conservation Corps programs managed by landscape architect Conrad L. Wirth, later to become Park Service director. Programs during this period shifted from a focus on natural sites to historic resources and parkways such as the Blue Ridge Parkway in Virginia and North Carolina and battlefields and historical parks such as Gettysburg in Pennsylvania.

Years of low funding and lack of interest left the national park system in a state of disrepair after World War II. Conrad Wirth proposed a major conservation program that would implement a nationwide effort to assess, reorganize and restore all parts of the park system. Known as Mission 66 and initiated in 1956 as a 10-year national park renewal, it led to significant federal support, which in turn raised the standards of all national parks. A planning staff, including three landscape architects headed by William Carnes, developed the program. Campgrounds were restored and sometimes even relocated to more appropriate sites (a campsite in Yellowstone National Park was discovered to have been located on the path of migrating grizzly bears), new roads and trails were built, visitor centers for the first time were established and management policies were instituted. By 1966 the park system had evolved fully into a nationally recognized network of parks.

In this time of explosive demands for use of the parks, the job of protecting fragile natural, historic, cultural and scenic resources has become increasingly complex for the National Park Service. There is probably no other governmental agency in which landscape architects have had more influence in this process. ✾

Ranger Club House, Yosemite National Park, an outstanding example of "parkitecture," a style of building design used in the national parks. (National Park Service)

Above: Gettysburg National Military Park, Pa., a historical park that benefited from Mission 66. (National Park Service)

Center: Thomas C. Vint, second from left, studying the master plan of a California park, 1931. (National Park Service)

NEW TOWNS AND PLANNED COMMUNITIES
Arnold R. Alanen

Every town and city was new at some time, and many were planned—even if merely for speculative purposes. The terms "new towns" and "planned communities," however, have come to refer to model villages, social utopias, garden cities, new communities and new towns-in-town. Landscape architects have played a key role in designing many of these developments.

Williamsburg, Philadelphia, Savannah, Washington, D.C., and other cities merit designation as 17th- and 18th-century new towns because of their rather unique design features. Also, several planned mill towns in New England—for example, Lowell, Mass. (1822), and Manchester, N.H. (1831)—ushered in America's industrial era during the early 19th century. Somewhat later, planned suburban communities emerged in Llewelyn Park, N.J. (1853), and Lake Forest (1857) and Riverside (1868–70), Ill. the latter designed by Olmsted and Vaux. The plans for these suburban communities incorporated curvilinear streets, ample open space and a unity between landscape and architecture characteristic of picturesque or romantic planning in mid-19th-century America.

From 1870 to 1930 most planned communities were suburban enclaves for wealthy Americans or corporate model villages. Suburban examples include three projects from the Olmsted office—Baltimore's Roland Park (1891), Forest Hills Gardens (1911), Queens, N.Y., and Palos Verdes Estates (1923) near Los Angeles—as well as Hare and Hare's Country Club District (1913–33) in Kansas City, Mo. Model industrial villages include Pullman, Ill. (1881); Olmsted's plan for Vandergrift, Pa. (1895); various schemes for Kohler, Wis. (1913–25), prepared by Hegemann and Peets and, later, the Olmsted firm; Morgan Park, Minn. (1913), developed by the Morell and Nichols partnership; John Nolen's proposals for Kingsport, Tenn. (1921–23); and layouts by Earle Draper for scores of southern mill villages including Chicopee, Ga. (1927).

Opposite: Kingsport, Tenn., a model industrial village designed by John Nolen. (Kingsport City Manager's Office)

Morgan Park, a company town in Duluth, Minn. (U.S. Steel Corporation, Bureau of Safety, Sanitation and Welfare)

Ebenezer Howard's diagram for a model garden city, which influenced many American communities. (Howard, *Garden Cities of To-morrow*, 1898)

Plan for Yorkship Village, Camden, N.J., 1918, combining City Beautiful principles and the curvilinearity of English garden cities. (A. C. Comey and M. S. Wehrly, *Planned Communities*, 1939)

Plan for Radburn, N.J. (Comey and Wehrly)

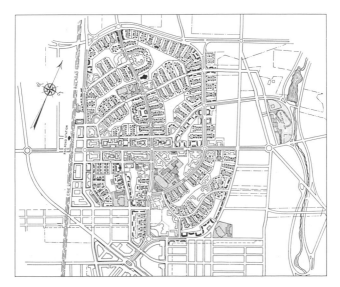

Opposite: Plan for Greenhills, Ohio, a New Deal community. (Archives, Cornell University Library)

Opposite center: Children in Greendale, Wis., 1939, another New Deal town. (Library of Congress)

After 1900 certain American planned communities incorporated some of the garden city principles espoused for England by Ebenezer Howard in 1898, although most American developments failed to preserve a permanent greenbelt or to achieve a mixture of social groups and land uses. Among the more successful American versions of garden cities were several communities sponsored by the federal government during World War I, but the foremost example of pre-1930s planning emerged at Radburn, N.J. (1928–29). Designed by architects Clarence Stein and Henry Wright and landscape architect Marjorie Cautley, the "Radburn idea" embraced several innovative concepts: designation of neighborhood units, clustering into superblocks, separate pedestrian and vehicular movement systems and park areas as the backbone for community design.

Community planning during the Depression featured the Tennessee Valley Authority enclave (1933) in Norris, Tenn., designed by Tracy Aguar, and three greenbelt towns (1935–38)—Greenbelt, Md. (Hale Walker), Greenhills, Ohio (Justin Hartzog and William A. Strong), and Greendale, Wis. (Elbert Peets and Jacob Crane)—sponsored by President Franklin D. Roosevelt's New Deal administration. They remain among the best-known versions of garden city planning in America, although most of the greenbelt acreage in the three eventually succumbed to development pressures. Later, housing needs after World War II led to the development of many large subdivisions, typified by the three Levittowns in New York (1947), Pennsylvania (1950) and New Jersey (1955).

By the 1960s, a new era of planned community development was launched with the planning of new towns of Reston, Va. (1964), and Columbia, Md. (1965). These two developments, as well as many others such as Irvine, Calif. (1964), Maumelle, Ark. (1967, Albert Mayer), Jonathan, Minn. (1967), Park Forest South, Ill. (1967), and the new towns-in-town of Cedar-Riverside (1971) in Minneapolis and Roosevelt Island (1972) in New York City often sought to incorporate some of the design features of planned communities emerging simultaneously in Europe, for example, the British new towns and Tapiola, Finland. All involved landscape architects, but none displayed a stronger sensitivity to contemporary ecological concerns than did the new town near Houston, Woodlands (1972, Wallace, McHarg, Roberts and Todd).

New town development in the United States has been most noticeable during periods of economic expansion or interest in large-scale planning (for example, the 1920s and 1960s). Today, other than some large subdivisions now appearing in rapid-growth areas of the United States, relatively few planned communities are being built. Undoubtedly, however, the idea will once again emerge as a significant planning movement. 🖋

Opposite left and above: Plan for Lake Anne Village, Reston, Va., and townhouses along the water's edge. The urbane plan coupled with the community's landscape features and housing made it one of the best-known new towns of the 1960s. (Alanen collection; Arnold Alanen)

PARKWAYS
Harley E. Jolley

"God grant me the serenity to accept the things I cannot change, courage to change the things I can and wisdom always to know the difference." This "alcoholics' prayer" easily could be that of landscape architects. They, too, have dreams of converting the ugly and devastating into the beautiful and exhilarating. Their demons are degraded environments. Their stimulants are marrying beauty and utility to create "the way more beautiful"—the parkway— for society's pleasure.

The late U.S. Senator Harry F. Byrd once captured the essence of a parkway: "It is a wonder way over which the tourist will ride comfortably in his car while he is stirred by a view as exhilarating as the aviator may see from the plane." To ensure that exhilaration, a parkway is designed for pleasure, artfully simulating nature's open spaces.

William Penn purportedly incorporated a parkway into his beloved Philadelphia, and Olmsted and Vaux's Central Park classically demonstrated the benefits of the pleasure way. But true parkways are a 20th-century phenomenon, twin-born with the automobile. The rural crest of the Blue Ridge Highway between Virginia and North Carolina gave birth to the idea in 1909. However, the suburban parkways of Westchester County, N.Y. (1913–38), were the mold into which most others have been cast.

Today's parkways are remarkably diverse in design and function, as exemplified by the George Washington Memorial (commemorative) and Colonial (historical) parkways in Virginia and Natchez Trace (heritage) Parkway in Mississippi, approved by Congress in 1928, 1930 and 1938, respectively (the three were the products of National Park Service design teams). All, however, continue objectives stated by the Westchester planners: "To preserve for

Opposite center: On the banks of the Bronx River, Tuckahoe, N.Y. Embodying the sense of leisure that the Westchester County parkways were meant to inspire, these painters in 1917 enjoy a pleasant afternoon near the Bronx River Parkway. (Westchester County, N.Y., Archives)

Bronx River Parkway, Yonkers, N.Y., 1922. (Westchester County, N.Y., Archives)

Boating on the flooded Bronx River, Yonkers, N.Y., 1914. (Westchester County, N.Y., Archives)

Below: Park along the Bronx River Parkway, Hartsdale, N.Y., 1916. (Westchester County, N.Y., Archives)

Center: Watering trees along the Bronx River Parkway, near Hartsdale, 1912. (Westchester County, N.Y., Archives)

present and future generations some of the charm and natural beauty . . . to provide for the refreshment of the mind
and body plus the well being and happiness of the people."
They share, too, the dictum of historian Hiram M. Chit-
tenden, designer of the Yellowstone National Park roads:
"They must lie lightly upon the ground." Common, also,
are motivations: easing a traffic headache, alleviating
inner-city deterioration, rehabilitating a polluted river basin or converting an environmental wasteland into a play-
land. Out of such considerations were born the Bronx River
Parkway of Westchester County, N.Y., and its sisters, the
Hutchinson River, Sawmill River and Cross County parkways. Likewise, the Blue Ridge Parkway in Virginia was a
Depression child, designed to rehabilitate people and land.

These two parkways—one metropolitan-suburban, the
other rural—provided prototypes for most others: curvilinear alignment, limited access, elimination of grade cross-
ings, exclusion of commercial traffic, satellite parks, scenic
easements, a consummate blending of natural and cultural
features, and the conversion of the entire corridor into a
park. Their landscape architects—Gilmore D. Clarke for
the Bronx River, begun in 1913, and Stanley W. Abbott for
the Blue Ridge, begun in 1935 and following the old Blue
Ridge Highway—worked with vastly different media:
Clarke with the leavings of many years of city despolia-
tion, Abbott with the jaded remnants of two centuries'
land abuse. But masterpieces emerged, classic models of
design, preservation and conservation.

Their legendary accomplishments inspired other parkways at the federal, state and regional levels, such as the
George Washington Memorial, Garden State (late 1940s) in
New Jersey and Mississippi River (planned in the mid-
1950s), constructed from Minnesota to Louisiana. All were
conservation, preservation and recreation oriented, designed to provide a new visual, mental and spiritual experience for a vast public exasperated with tension-producing
commuter ways. All sought to create what Abbott called
"rare gems in the necklace." Thanks to their visionary
skills, millions today are able to say, joyfully, "Let's take a
break and go on the parkway!" 🞋

Opposite bottom and below: Colonial Parkway in Virginia, 1936, and Civilian Conservation Corps enrollees planting trees along the parkway.
(National Park Service, Colonial National Historical Park Archives)

Linville River Bridge, part of the Blue Ridge Parkway in North Carolina. (National Park Service, Blue Ridge Parkway Archives)

Pastoral scene along the Blue Ridge Parkway, 1952. (National Park Service, Blue Ridge Parkway Archives)

Vista House (1918) on Crown Point and the Columbia River Gorge off the Columbia River Highway in Oregon, a parkway offering spectacular western scenery. (Jim Norman, Oregon State Highway Division)

Landscape Architect's Lake along the Blue Ridge Parkway in Virginia.
(National Park Service, Blue Ridge Parkway Archives)

RECREATIONAL AREAS
Miriam Easton Rutz

Of the endless range of recreational activities, many take place in an attractive landscape setting. Arboretums and zoological gardens of kings and nobility in Egypt, Mesopotamia and Mexico, as well as places of leisure in many other cultures, have long been described in literature. Taking a cue from their classical Roman ancestors, the Italians in the 16th century and the French in the 17th and 18th centuries built luxurious dwellings on extensive landscaped grounds that served as settings for recreation and amusement. In the American colonies, the gardens of southern plantations were developed for pleasure and leisure activities.

As cities grew, open space for recreation became more difficult to find. Cemeteries, with their parklike settings, turned into popular places for picnics and strolls. Urban, national and state parks were developed to provide areas for people to spend their leisure time. However, public spaces did not offer all the desired recreational facilities, and, with the increasing prosperity enjoyed in the United States from the mid-19th century, private, sometimes nonprofit organizations began providing additional parks, zoos, gardens, resorts, clubs and camps.

Traditionally, landscape architects have been involved in the design of these recreational areas, because planning is needed to accommodate people while protecting the existing environment. In zoos, for example, the creation of an animal's proper ecological setting or exhibits combining a region's plant and animal collections have become important contemporary concepts. Exposition and world's fair grounds such as Balboa Park (1926) in San Diego were early examples of recreational spaces that incorporated parks, cultural events and amusement areas. Many of their design characteristics can be recognized in now-popular theme parks, including a prominent view of an important structure from the entry gate, well-planned circulating patterns and consideration for visitor comfort.

The natural environment and vistas are important in planning resorts and clubs. Clubs usually focus on one or

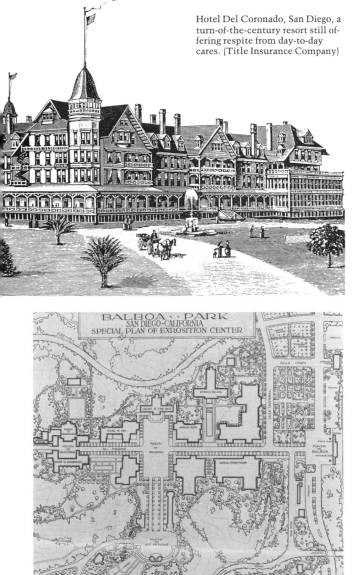

Hotel Del Coronado, San Diego, a turn-of-the-century resort still offering respite from day-to-day cares. (Title Insurance Company)

Plan for Balboa Park, San Diego, by John Nolen, an exposition site with features recognizable in today's theme parks. (Archives, Cornell University Library)

two primary activities such as golf, tennis, swimming, boating, horseback riding or skiing, combined with a dining facility or clubhouse. Resorts usually have a combination of housing units including hotels, condominiums and second homes, along with recreational activities. Because such places are set in locations of natural beauty, the search for the proper setting is a major task. The Grand Hotel (1887) on Mackinac Island, Mich., and the Hotel Del Coronado (1888) near San Diego are good examples of turn-of-the-century resorts that still maintain their original purpose. Resorts created today such as the Homestead near Traverse City, Mich., designed by Johnson, Johnson and Roy in the early 1970s, are carefully planned to provide

Animal enclosure at the Sonora Desert Museum, Tucson. Recessed animal enclosures permit unobstructed views of the desert. (Tim Fuller)

much more for the visitor, along with landscaped grounds and carefully protected natural features.

Recreation entails rejuvenation of the spirit as well as the body, so outdoor spaces for recreation must refresh the whole person. This requires using land, water, plants, views, breezes and other site amenities. But recreation often also calls for fantasy and nostalgia—places such as the turn-of-the-century Main Street at Disneyland (1957), the ethnic farms at Old World Wisconsin (1976) and the varied geographical settings at Seattle's Woodland Park Zoo, redesigned in the late 1970s by Jones and Jones, also testify to the landscape architect's role in maximizing planned recreational experiences. 🍂

Opposite: Finnish farmstead at the Old World Wisconsin outdoor museum. Meticulous research into building types and landscape features led to the museum's displays, which provide enjoyment and education for millions of Americans who seek out such historical museums for recreation. (Hanque Macari; Tishler collection)

Gorilla yard at the Great Ape House, National Zoological Park, Washington, D.C. Such "cageless" enclosures enhance visitors' perceptions of an animal's environment. (Jessie Cohen)

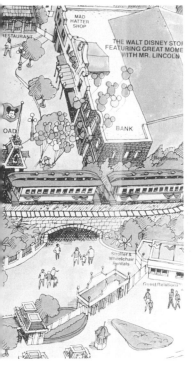

Preparatory drawing for Disneyland, Anaheim, Calif., where a nostalgia for latter-day Main Streets, an important theme, attracts park visitors.

RESTORED NATURAL LANDSCAPES
Darrel G. Morrison

Natural landscape restoration—the process of returning a site's natural, presettlement character—is one of several strategies for restoring landscapes. Others involve reverting to conditions found during a site's cultural evolution, such as an earlier agricultural stage, and re-creating a design plan implemented in the past. Any of these scenarios involves the manipulation of vegetation, including the removal of uncharacteristic plants and the reintroduction of representative species.

Natural restoration aims to reestablish native species found before human settlement, replicating the species composition, diversity and distribution patterns. True natural restoration is rarely if ever achieved because of our inability to re-create all the former conditions on a disturbed site. Thus, a practical definition of natural landscape restoration is the reestablishment of native species in community-like groupings on sites that can be expected to sustain them. This definition can encompass work ranging from small native gardens to large parks and open spaces. Ideally, a multidisciplinary approach involving a botanist-ecologist and a landscape architect is followed.

Perhaps the most renowned landscape architect who demonstrated landscape restoration in America was Jens Jensen, particularly in his Chicago park work. From the late 19th century until the 1940s, this emphasis became his central theme, as in his "prairie river" in Chicago's Columbus Park in 1918 and in Lincoln Memorial Garden, Springfield, Ill., designed in 1936. Jensen was influenced by Henry Cowles, a botanist with whom he frequently explored natural landscapes in Illinois and northern Indiana. Jensen's natural restoration work was acknowledged to be a stylized version of nature. He wisely noted that one cannot copy nature but can, through careful observation, learn its "motives" and aesthetic essence and incorporate these into designed concepts.

Another important landscape restoration team consisted of Edith A. Roberts, a plant ecologist, and landscape architect Elsa Rehmann. In their book *American Plants for American Gardens* (1929), they promoted the use of native American plants in groupings based on natural plant communities. The book provided underlying ecological concepts and also recommended lists of native plant species for use in landscape designs.

While other landscape architects undoubtedly practiced native landscape restoration from the 1930s to the 1960s, it was not a major focus of the profession during that period. With the advent of Earth Day in 1970, however, natural landscape restoration concepts reemerged as an area of the profession's theory and practice. During the 1970s the ecological and aesthetic potential of plant community restorations was demonstrated on a variety of sites in the midwestern Tallgrass Prairie region. These included residential and corporate sites in Wisconsin designed by the author; the Kansas City, Mo., airport entrance road (1973, Fred Markham and Associates) and a number of roadside prairie restoration projects orchestrated by highway departments in the Midwest. In the Northeast, Andropogon Associates has included natural landscape restorations as part of its ecological planning and design services, using the deciduous forest and eastern meadow as models.

Sunny meadow in Lincoln Memorial Garden, Springfield, Ill., designed by Jens Jensen, an early proponent of the use of native vegetation. (Jensen Collection, Morton Arboretum)

Streamside restoration, Lincoln Memorial Garden. (Darrel G. Morrison)

Planting near the Kansas City, Mo., International Airport. Travelers know they are in prairie country when they see these native grasses and wildflowers. (Darrel G. Morrison)

The art of restoring natural lands implies first an understanding of the natural landscape and native communities of a region; then an ability to simplify and stylize without losing the aesthetic essence of these complex systems in a designed environment; and knowledge of plant propagation and establishment techniques. Finally, it requires an understanding that natural landscapes, particularly restored natural landscapes, require intelligent management to perpetuate dynamic natural character while maintaining designed spatial configurations. 🌿

Native grasses such as switchgrass, Indian grass and little bluestem with native flowers planted for the General Electric Medical Systems site, Waukesha County, Wis. (Darrel G. Morrison)

Right, opposite and below: Environmental protection and restoration following installation of a natural gas pipeline through a Morris County, N.J., park. To the right, stream banks are stabilized at the pipeline crossing, while flow is maintained in flume pipes.

Little bluestem, Indian grass, purple cornflower and other native prairie species filling a sunny slope near the offices of CUNA Mutual Insurance, Madison, Wis. (Darrel G. Morrison)

Stream banks regraded to natural contours after the pipeline was fully installed.

Native wetland vegetation fully reclaiming site after six months. (All, Leslie Sauer and Carol Franklin, Andropogon Associates)

Top: McCormick's Creek State
Park, Ind., typifying the "grand"
scenery of the classic state parks
from the founding period. (Indiana
Division of State Parks)

Above: Chimney Bluffs, upper
New York State, an undeveloped
park reflecting the fascination
with exotic land forms. (New York
State Department of Commerce)

STATE PARKS
Phoebe Cutler

State parks as scenic areas reserved for public recreation are
one of our great open space resources. Although the total
state parkland mass is one-seventh that of the national
parks, these state preserves receive more than twice as
many visitors. A wide variety exists among state parks,
states and even parks within a single state. Yosemite,
ceded to California in 1864 by President Abraham Lincoln,
set the standard for spectacular natural scenery that was to
guide state park selection for the first half of its history.
Yosemite later reverted to the federal government, but not
before inspiring such early outstanding parks as the Pali-
sades (1900) and Watkins Glen (1906) in New York,
Starved Rock (1911) in Illinois and Mt. Mitchell (1915) in
North Carolina. All these parks show the geological
uniqueness that Frederick Law Olmsted, Jr., was to cite in
1928 as the "fundamental determinant" for choosing a site.

The evolution of the state park falls broadly into three
periods. During the founding phase from the 1880s to
1921, a few states, notably New York, Connecticut, Indiana, Iowa and Wisconsin, selected sites as uniquely worth
preserving. The next period, from 1921 to 1942, saw the
spread of state parks throughout the country and the rise of
park systems. Finally, the postwar or modern period has
witnessed a tripling of state parkland area.

Yosemite served as a model for the founding period, although a premature one, because the next state parks, including Niagara Falls (1885) in New York and Mackinac Island (1885) in Michigan, were not established for another
20 years. Significant growth did not occur until after World
War I. Michigan launched its system in 1919, creating 23
parks in two years. Yet, at the end of the founding phase,
29 states lacked a single park and six had only one each.

The next 20 years saw state parks become a common fix-
ture, first through individual state initiatives and then
through federal sponsorship backed by the labor of the Civilian Conservation Corps. As an active director of the
state with the earliest and greatest number of parks, New
York's Robert Moses exerted great influence on modern
state park development throughout this period and into the
next. His emphasis on recreation over conservation made
the parks more utilitarian and opened the way for the now-
prevalent diversification of facilities and functions.

Today, state governments are developing existing parks
rather than acquiring new parklands. A period of retrench-
ment has replaced the expansion that occurred from 1918
to the late 1970s. In the Southeast the digression into
"state resort parks" with golf courses, swimming pools and
convention facilities has aimed to boost local economies.
The lure of the tourist dollar, coupled with the need for in-
come, is tempting other regions to build inns and expand
recreational facilities. Despite this tendency toward a historically anomalous sophistication, camping still is by far
the predominant mode of lodging; after camping fees, sales
of soft drinks bring in the most revenue.

Both the proliferation and commercialization of state
parks have meant a sapping of the original concentration
on outstanding scenery, but state parks continue to provide, first and foremost, quiet diversion in a natural setting, with picnicking, hiking and swimming still the principal occupations. 🖋

Seashore State Park, Va., the
state's first proposed park and its
most popular. Such parks have
been the principal means of securing public access to prime ocean
beaches. (Virginia Division of
Parks and Recreation)

Racoon Creek State Park, Pa., created to rehabilitate land and establish extensive recreational areas
during the Depression. (Pennsylvania Bureau of State Parks)

Petit Jean State Park lodge, Ark., built by the Civilian Conservation
Corps during the 1930s in a rustic style typical of architecture in many
parks. (National Park Service)

La Purisima Mission State Historic Park, Lompoc, Calif., exemplifying the state park as historical preserve. The mission was restored by the CCC. (California Department of Parks and Recreation)

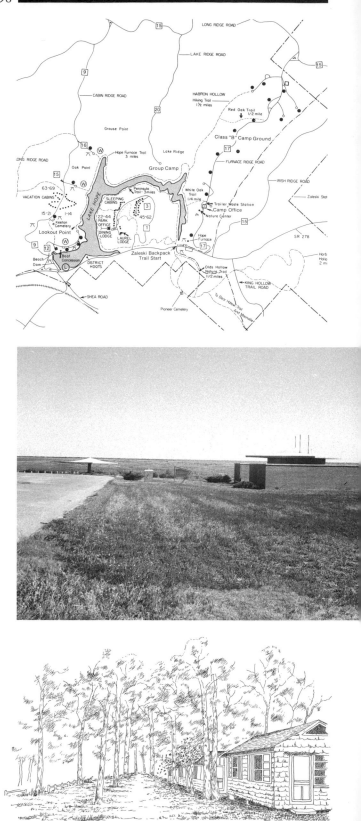

Norris Dam State Resort Park, Tenn. Cabins are located in 29 state parks, most of which are in the South. (Madelaine Gill Linden)

Opposite: Map of Lake Hope State Park, Ohio, a typical layout, with cabins built by the CCC. (Ohio Division of Parks and Recreation)

Lake Barkeley, a resort park in Kentucky with increased facilities to attract more visitors. (Kentucky Department of Parks)

Prairie Dog State Park, Kans. Here the once requisite woodland is gone, but the all-important lake persists. (Phoebe Cutler)

Norris Dam State Resort Park. At least 40 years and widely different philosophies separate these cabins from those on the opposite page. (Madelaine Gill Linden)

STREETSCAPES, SQUARES AND PLAZAS
Mark Chidister

Medieval and Renaissance European cities were the pattern for many colonial town plans and squares in America—a pattern freely adjusted to frontier realities and aspirations. European influences are still apparent in some town plans and squares. However, recent dramatic changes in urban growth and form have left an imprint of streets and plazas that are as different from their European counterparts as today's Americans are from their ancestors.

Closest to the planned towns of medieval Europe were the Spanish colonial settlements. These settlements were planned and organized on a grid around a regular, central plaza. The remnants of two such plazas remain in Santa Fe (1609) and Albuquerque (1781). Like their medieval counterparts, such plazas were the spatial, political, commercial, social and often religious focus of the community—essential places, not amenities. In contrast to the uniformity of Spanish town plans, French and English settlements varied in form. While gridiron plans predominated, a wide variety of street patterns were built. Invariably, a public green space such as the New Haven Green (1638) in Connecticut was included. These commons and residential squares were used for grazing animals, parades, militia assemblies, ornamental gardens and settings for churches and town halls. Early public squares in the United States, in contrast to private residential squares of London and Paris, became symbols of a new egalitarian society. Yet none achieved the diversity and intensity of use found in Spanish colonial or European medieval squares. Rather, vital functions focused on main streets of small towns and districts of large cities.

The rapid growth of cities during the late 19th and early 20th centuries was not accompanied by significant increases in central-city open space. Unlike European cities, where density was balanced by abundant plazas, American cities after World War II were complex, crowded places

...

New Haven Green, New Haven, Conn., c. 1884–89, an open area traditionally included in early French and English settlements. (New Haven Colony Historical Society)

Public Square, Cleveland, 1859, representative of a new egalitarian society. (Zucker, *Town and Square*, 1959)

with little or no spatial relief. A half century earlier the World's Columbian Exposition in Chicago had projected the dream of cities with grand streets and generous squares—a dream largely unrealized.

Faced with this lack of open space, city planners in the 1950s and 1960s devised incentive zoning to encourage private development with plazas for public use. Despite the opportunities these new plazas afforded, there were costs: shaded streets from taller buildings, uncoordinated open space patterns and plazas sometimes catering more to private interests than public good.

While corporate skyscraper plazas have dominated the scene since the 1960s, many civic and commerical plazas and streetscapes have been undertaken to make downtowns more habitable and desirable. Two adaptive use projects, Ghirardelli Square (1962, Wurster, Bernardi and Emmons, with Lawrence Halprin and Associates) in San Francisco and Fanueil Hall Marketplace (1976–78, Benjamin Thompson Associates) in Boston are privately owned and managed but receive an intensity and diversity

Seagram Building (1957, Ludwig Mies van der Rohe), New York City, which broke new ground for the skyscraper-plaza ensembles to follow. (John Burgee Architects)

Outdoor cafe, Faneuil Hall Marketplace, Boston, a model for many festival marketplaces. (© Steve Rosenthal)

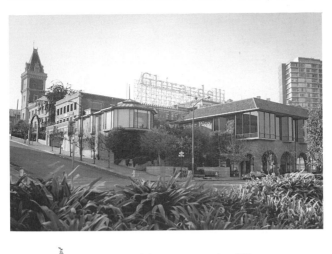

Top and above: Ghirardelli Square, San Francisco, a two-and-one-half acre adaptive use project developed around a candy factory. The sign is an old harbor landmark. (Joshua Freiwald; George Albertus, Ghirardelli Square)

of use that few corporate plazas have generated. Recent civic plazas range from the brick expanse of Boston's City Hall Plaza (1968, Kallman, McKinnell and Knowles) to the complexity of Minneapolis's Peavy Plaza (1975, M. Paul Friedburg and Partners) and the Auditorium Forecourt Fountain (1970, Lawrence Halprin) in Portland, Ore. On the whole, recent plazas have become dispersed local spaces centered around young office workers, weekday lunches and planned events. Most streetscape projects serve as downtown open-air shopping malls to make working and shopping enjoyable. Many, like Nicollet Mall (1968–81, Lawrence Halprin) in Minneapolis and the State Street Mall (1975–81, M. Paul Friedburg) in Madison, Wis., have done well. Some less successful malls are being demolished and replaced with standard streets and sidewalks.

Plazas and streets are being transformed. New "public" spaces are increasingly indoors and privately managed. The Ford Foundation atrium (1967, Dan Kiley) in New York City was an oddity when built. It is now the staple. Atriums, arcades, galleries, courts and skywalks abound, and traditional street life is moving indoors. Despite their pleasures and opportunities, they have not served as common spaces for the public. In a time when there is renewed interest in cities and public life, care must be taken to perpetuate and add places to our cities where access and use by all of the public are ensured. ✍

Boston City Hall Plaza, inspired by the paved piazzas of medieval Italy.
(© 1988 Cervin Robinson)

Auditorium Forecourt Fountain, Portland, Ore., based on principles of
improvisational theater and environmental art to encourage spontane-
ous activity. (Mark Chidister)

Atrium, Ford Foundation Headquarters, New York City, the genesis of numerous new interior urban spaces. (© 1967 Ezra Stoller/Esto)

Nicollet Mall, Minneapolis, a model pedestrian outdoor mall served by public transportation. (Mark Chidister)

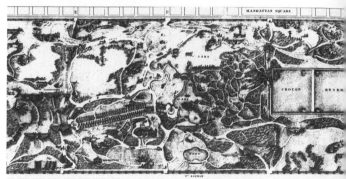

URBAN PARKS
Anne Whiston Spirn

The first parks were royal hunting grounds. The word "park" itself meant an enclosed tract of land for keeping beasts of the chase and, later, deer, cattle and sheep. The Boston Common, set aside as common pasture in 1630, was America's first public park. From these origins in animal husbandry and stewardship, the park became associated with the health of both people and the city itself—as if a park were "the lungs of the city."

Other early American "parks" were town squares. William Penn's plan for Philadelphia in 1683, for example, and James Oglethorpe's plan for Savannah in 1733 set aside squares that were ultimately surrounded by residences and institutions. These represented a vision of urbanity inspired by new town planning ideas in England.

All across America, for a half century from 1858 on, cities built large urban parks, designed in a pastoral style: Central Park (1858, Olmsted and Vaux) in New York City; Fairmount Park (1865) in Philadelphia; Forest Park (1876) in St. Louis; Golden Gate Park (1870) in San Francisco.

By the end of the 19th century, the park stood for certain democratic ideals. Frederick Law Olmsted, for example, saw the park as common ground where all citizens might have access to "the best scenery of the region." This idea found its expression in Olmsted's work in Boston on what sometimes is referred to as the Emerald Necklace (1878–95). One of the nation's first and most completely developed urban park systems, it connected the heart of the city with new suburbs and outlying farmland and integrated parks and parkways with a streetcar line and storm drainage. As systems, parks shaped the growth of American cities, inspired the city planning movement in the United States and increased adjacent land values, contributing to the city's economic health.

The large 19th-century parks have been adapted again and again to meet changing needs and values. As American society has changed, so have the role and form of the urban park. Older urban parks are now composed of layers of erasures and additions. Many have been sites of expositions, whose buildings still remain; others have accommodated the addition of facilities for intensive recreation, such as stadiums, skating rinks and swimming pools.

Sports and games became an increasingly important part of parks during the 20th century. Charlesbank (1892, Frederick Law Olmsted) in Boston was among the first urban playgrounds. By the 1920s metropolitan parks such as New

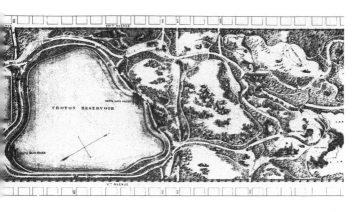

Above: Charlesbank from West Boston Bridge, c. 1890, one of the nation's first playgrounds. (Harvard University)

Top: Plan for Central Park, New York City, originally surrounded by fields. (National Park Service, Olmsted NHS)

York's Jones Beach (1929, Long Island Park Commission) were built for the recreational needs of enormous numbers of city residents who arrived not by streetcar, but by automobile. Since the development of the Emerald Necklace in the last century, parks have often been associated with transportation projects. The esplanade of Carl Schurz Park in New York City is cantilevered out over the East River with a highway on the lower level.

We owe many urban parks to a concern for health and safety. The establishment of Fairmount Park in Philadelphia was motivated, in part, by a desire to protect the city's water supply, the Boston system's Fens and Riverway by a plan to improve water quality and reduce floods. The San Antonio Riverwalk (1939–41) was also a response to a flood hazard.

Today, urban parks range from tiny "pocket" parks to entire districts. Paley Park (1965–68, Zion and Breen) in New York City, the size of a single building lot, is an oasis in midtown Manhattan. Independence National Historical Park (1956) in Philadelphia includes historic buildings as well as plazas, landscaped blocks and gardens. More recently, entire portions of cities in need of economic revital-

Conservatory of Flowers in Golden Gate Park (1870–c. 1910), a 1,017-acre area encompassing 12 lakes and many gardens. (Clarence Towers, Golden Gate Park)

Above: Carl Shurz Park, New York City. The promenade is a roof garden over a drive. (Rodney McCay Morgan/Parks Archive)

Center: Jones Beach, Long Island, N.Y., designed for the automobile age. (Long Island State Park Commission)

Independence National Historical Park, Philadelphia, a comprehensive project involving urban renewal, historic preservation, interpretation and recreational development. (National Park Service)

ization have been designated as parks: Lowell National Historical Park (1978) in Lowell, Mass., for example.

The park has been an extremely fertile idea that has continued to evolve and to spawn many other landscape types such as the parkway, the garden suburb, the playground, the amusement park and the industrial park. Today, urban parks carry with them many associations: stewardship, health, scenery, sport, economic revitilization and the framework for human settlement. These responsibilities are a complex burden for a single type of open space to fulfill and present a challenge for plotting the present and future role of the urban park in American society. ✍

WATERFRONTS
Roy B. Mann

During the second half of the 19th century, the park movement, which had demonstrated how recreational and civic
needs could be met through the provision of parklands,
grew and found expression on shore with designed public
waterfronts. Frederick Law Olmsted pioneered several
forms of waterfront parks, among them the parkway-edged
Muddy River segments of Boston's urban park system
(1878–95), known as the Emerald Necklace, residential
amenity shoreland in Riverside, Ill. (1868–70), and, most
spectacularly, waterfront exhibition grounds such as the
1893 World's Columbian Exposition in Chicago. The latter
set the cornerstones for Chicago's quintessential lakefront
park system and helped launch the City Beautiful movement that nurtured civic development well into the 20th
century.

Charles Eliot helped shape several recreational waterfronts, including the seaside Revere Beach Reservation
(1896) in Revere, Mass. Eliot and other landscape architects, including Olmsted, discovered that both coastal and
river parklands could be imbued with naturalism in design,
responding to the inherent qualities of the American waterfront environment. But the Beaux Arts influence of the
City Beautiful movement was active as well. It introduced
Renaissance-inspired embellishments such as the Charles
River basin's balustraded edgings and boat landings (1929,
Arthur A. Shurtleff [later Shurcliff], et al.) in Boston; long,
formal promenades such as that of Manhattan's Riverside
Park (1868–89, Olmsted and Vaux); and such classical
structures as the Jefferson Memorial (1943, John Russell
Pope) in Washington, D.C., where the Tidal Basin, on
which the memorial is sited, was planted with Japanese
flowering cherries and other landscape materials in 1912
under the direction of landscape architect George E.
Burnap.

After World War II, and particularly with the development of the interstate highway system in the 1950s, industry and warehousing abandoned many inner-city waterfronts, creating new potential for public access and leisure
areas. At the same time, abandonment and industrial
abuse produced serious aesthetic and environmental
impacts.

Facing new challenges posed by these transitional waterfronts and the need to accommodate the open space and

Opposite: Point State Park (1945, GWSM, Inc.), Pittsburgh, poised at the confluence of the Allegheny and Monongahela rivers as they form the Ohio.

Boston's Charles River basin, America's premier urban recreational waterway, during the Head-of-the-Charles regatta. (Roy B. Mann)

Gas Works Park (1973, Richard Haag Associates), Seattle, where the artifacts of industrial archeology have been turned into a playground contrasting with verdant shoreland.

Paseo del Rio, San Antonio, a crowd-pleasing riverfront. Floodgates prevent floodwaters from reaching this one-mile horseshoe bend. (San Antonio Convention and Visitors Bureau)

recreational needs of growing urban and suburban populations, landscape architects and planners worked in the 1950s and early 1960s to replace blighted waterfronts with parks and other open space, some in conjunction with new civic facilities. Many broke with classical traditions and introduced contemporary design elements. Most sought to provide passive and quiet spaces as relief from the urban realm. Some attempted to emulate the waterfronts of Europe, but the Old World influence would not have a true impact until later in the 1960s.

In 1969 San Antonio's Hemisfair exposition brought national attention to the city's Paseo del Rio, or Riverwalk, a one-mile reach of open-air cafes, restaurants, shops and hotels conceived in the 1930s by architect Robert Huggeman as a simulation of a typical Spanish town form. With this example, with growing public support for historic preservation and adaptive use as seen in Boston's Faneuil Hall Marketplace (1976–78, Benjamin Thompson Associates) and with growing public interest in social and cultural activity in public places, the corner was turned toward the more vibrant waterfront of the 1970s and 1980s.

A fascination with Europe's unique public spaces and waterfronts had been communicated to Americans by numerous observers in the 1960s, including Lawrence Halprin in his book *Cities* (1963) and Britain's Gordon Cullen with his equally expressive *Townscape* (1961). In coastal cities, lakeshore communities and river towns, momentum grew for creating informal, marketplace-compatible and crowd-accommodating spaces by the water. Designers emulated European and Japanese attention to details and architectural idioms. New paving features, marine bollards, historical sign motifs, port-styled lamps and other harbor-related accoutrements came into use. The simulation of European waterfronts became not only desirable but feasible, while materials and forms were used

Harborplace, Baltimore, with its popular market pavilions in the background. Broad walkways along the harbor's edge accommodate large crowds and encourage an unhurried pace. (Rouse Company)

with growing originality to achieve an increasingly recognizable American waterfront idiom.

Along with Boston, other cities also reclaimed their historic waterfronts as public space opening the door to residential, retail and institutional activities. Baltimore's Inner Harbor restoration (1974, Wallace, McHarg, Roberts and Todd) included the market pavilions of Harborplace (1980, Benjamin Thompson Associates). Coastal areas were designed with the character of early American waterfronts, as, for example, at Hilton Head Island's Harbour Town (1970, Sasaki, Dawson, Demay Associates). Some canal-theme developments, Las Colinas in Dallas, for instance, echoed Venetian precedents.

The search for contemporary water-related forms has been carried out with increasing creativity. Riverbank Park (1979, CHNMB Associates) in Flint, Mich., introduced an Archimedes screw and flume as central elements in a geometric, sculptured scheme. In Tulsa, Okla., Athena Tacha's Blair Fountain (1982) created a unique combination of dam, waterfalls and sculpture with light and water displays. Ottawa's Rideau Canal, developed over many years, blended new park, restaurant and institutional edges with its traditional waterway and locks. Cincinnati's Serpentine (1975, Zion and Breen) created a dramatic water's edge highly compatible with the Ohio River's flood menace. The commitment to preserve a waterfront's environmental resources was dramatically expressed at the Sea Ranch residential project in Sonoma County, Calif. (1967, Lawrence Halprin and Associates), which broadened public perception of the fragility of coastal landscapes and their site design considerations.

Today, increasing design innovation, preservation of historic features and social and cultural enrichment of public space have become new strengths as waterfronts are reclaimed. These qualities may have come to stay. ✍

Opposite: Sea Ranch, Sonoma County, Calif., a landmark because it demonstrated that structures expressive of coastal land forms could appear both distinctive and subordinate to those forms. (Lawrence Halprin and Associates)

Brenke River Sculpture and Fish Ladder (1983, O'Boyle, Cowell, Blalock), Lansing, Mich. The project, in a downtown linear park, part of the state's effort to establish salmon as a game fish, created stairs for salmon returning upstream and stairs for visitors within concentric rings. (City of Lansing)

Cincinnati's Serpentine, demonstrating that flood control structures need not be restricted in design but can assume unique forms suited to both hydraulic flow and public enjoyment. (Paul L. Wertheimer)

Contributors

Arnold R. Alanen is professor of landscape architecture at the University of Wisconsin, Madison. He has served as coeditor of *Landscape Journal* and is coauthor of *Main Street Ready-Made: The New Deal Community of Greendale, Wisconsin*. His recent research has been devoted to documenting the physical form and social organization of company towns in the Lake Superior region.

Cheryl Barton, ASLA, is director of the EDAW Design Group in San Francisco, which has designed and constructed numerous corporate landscapes. She served as president of the American Society of Landscape Architects, 1987–88.

William L. Beiswanger is architectural historian and director of restoration for Monticello, Charlottesville, Va., where his responsibilities include documenting the design and construction of Monticello as well as developing and coordinating a program for the restoration of the house and re-creation of Thomas Jefferson's landscape.

Shary Page Berg, ASLA, is a landscape preservation consultant and instructor with the Radcliffe Seminars, Radcliffe College, Cambridge, Mass. She is also active in the Alliance for Historic Landscape Preservation.

Charles E. Beveridge is series editor of the Frederick Law Olmsted Papers, Department of History, The American University, Washington, D.C. He has lectured widely on Frederick Law Olmsted's landscape design career and is a historical consultant for several historic park and landscape restoration programs. He is also writing a book on Olmsted's theory and practice of landscape architecture.

Malcolm Cairns, ASLA, is associate professor of landscape architecture at Ball State University, Muncie, Ind., where his research focuses on historic parks and park communities. He is preparing an illustrated resource inventory of historic designed landscapes in Illinois.

Mark Chidister is associate professor of landscape architecture at Iowa State University, Ames. He is author of "The Effect of Context on the Use of Urban Plazas" (*Landscape Journal*) and "Reconsidering the Piazza" (*Landscape Architecture*) and is interested in public spaces and public life in America.

Stephen Christy, ASLA, is executive director of the Lake Forest Open Lands Association, a private nonprofit land conservation group active north of Chicago. A landscape architect, his prior work includes master planning, design and construction of a variety of projects in the Midwest.

Leslie Rose Close, ASLA, is director of the American Garden and Landscape History Program at Wave Hill in New York City. She also serves as codirector of the Catalog of Landscape Records in the United States.

Walter L. Creese, Hon. AIA, is author of *The Search for Environment, Nature and the Victorian Imagination* and *The Crowning of the American Landscape*. He is also professor emeritus of the School of Architecture, University of Illinois, Champaign-Urbana.

Phoebe Cutler, ASLA, is a landscape designer living in San Francisco. She is author of *The Public Landscape of the New Deal* and a recipient of the 1988 Rome Prize in the Design Arts.

Richard P. Dober, AICP, has served as a campus planning and design consultant to more than 300 colleges and universities worldwide and has written many articles, books and reviews about college and university architecture and landscape.

Julius Gy. Fabos, FASLA, is professor of landscape architecture and regional planning and director of the graduate program in landscape architecture at the University of Massachusetts, Amherst. He has lectured widely and is the author of more than 100 publications, including *Planning the Total Landscape* and *Land Use Planning: From Global to Local Challenge*.

Raymond L. Freeman, FASLA, a landscape architect and planning consultant, is a former deputy director of the National Park Service, past president of the American Society of Landscape Architects (1971–73) and recipient of the Interior Department's Distinguished Service Award and ASLA's Presidential Award. He is also a consultant to the American Society of Landscape Architects on government affairs and a senior delegate to the International Federation of Landscape Architects.

Robert E. Grese, ASLA, is assistant professor of landscape architecture at the University of Michigan, Ann Arbor. He has researched the early use of native plant communities by landscape architects and is writing a book on the work of Jens Jensen.

William Grundmann, ASLA, is associate professor of landscape architecture at Iowa State University, Ames, where he is curator of the Warren H. Manning Collection. He has researched Manning's work throughout the United States. He is editing a book of essays by a number of authors on Manning, his practice and his influence.

John L. Hancock is professor of urban design and planning at the University of Washington, Seattle. He has written extensively on John Nolen and is working on a biography of the planner, his firm and his times.

Kenneth I. Helphand, ASLA, is professor of landscape architecture at the University of Oregon, Eugene, and reviews editor of *Landscape Architecture*. A regular contributor to design journals, he is author of the forthcoming book *The Green Path: A History of Landscape Architecture*.

Catherine M. Howett, ASLA, is associate professor in the School of Environmental Design at the University of Georgia, Athens. She is a historian of 19th- and 20th-century American landscape architecture and is writing a book on the history of residential design.

Wayne D. Iverson, FASLA, spent 28 years with the U.S. Forest Service, the last 20 as regional landscape architect in the southern and western United States. He has long been interested in the history of landscape architects in that agency and is currently a consultant and principal of Scenic Resource Management in Sedona, Ariz.

Jory Johnson, ASLA, is a landscape designer and author of numerous publications on landscape design and environmental art. He is a lecturer at North Carolina State University, Raleigh, teaches at the College of Architecture, University of North Carolina, Charlotte, and is a contributing editor of *Landscape Architecture*.

Harley E. Jolley, Hon. ASLA, is professor of history at Mars Hill College, Mars Hill, N.C. An expert on the Blue Ridge Parkway, he has worked for the National Park Service, published widely and received numerous awards for his work.

Brian S. Kubota, FASLA, is co-owner and vice president of the multidisciplinary firm PKG Design Group, Lawrence, Kans. President of the firm's subsidiary, Landplan Engineering, he has been responsible for projects involving every aspect of landscape architecture and planning. A major project is the Alvamar Planned Community in Lawrence. He became president of the American Society of Landscape Architects in 1988.

Michael Laurie, FASLA, is professor of landscape architecture at the University of California, Berkeley. He is author of *An Introduction to Landscape Architecture*.

Arleyn A. Levee is a landscape historian and designer in Belmont, Mass. She is a consultant to the Massachusetts Olmsted Historic Landscape Preservation Program, working in Fall River, Mass. Active in numerous landscape preservation organizations, she is writing a biography of John Charles Olmsted.

Blanche Linden-Ward is assistant professor and coordinator of the American Culture Program at Emerson College, Boston. She is author of *Silent City on a Hill: Landscapes of Memory*, and *Boston's Mount Auburn Cemetery* and several articles on cemeteries, as well as the documentary video *Nature by Design: The Art and Landscape of Cincinnati's Spring Grove Cemetery*. Recipient of the American Society of Landscape Architects' 1985 Bradford Williams Award, she is working on a book on landscape change at Mount Auburn over the last 150 years.

Eleanor M. McPeck is an instructor in landscape history at the Radcliffe Seminars, Radcliffe College, Cambridge, Mass., and is a practicing landscape consultant with offices in Boston and Washington, D.C. She is a former Dumbarton Oaks Garden Fellow and coauthor of *Beatrix Farrand's American Landscapes: Her Gardens and Campuses*. She has written several articles on American landscape designers and subjects.

Roy B. Mann, ASLA, a former Fulbright scholar, heads the landscape architectural firm of RMA/Texas, Inc., in Austin, Tex., and has long been concerned with the planning of rivers, coasts and city waterfront areas. His book *Rivers in the City*, on waterfronts in urban regions of Europe and the United States, brought the potential for improved waterfront design into sharper public focus.

Roger B. Martin, FASLA, is professor of landscape architecture at the University of Minnesota, Minneapolis, and past president of the American Society of Landscape Architects (1986–88). His focus on the role and responsibility of the landscape architect in public open space has resulted in studies of park facilities throughout the United States. As principal with Martin and Pitz Associates, he has designed large-scale open space systems in the upper Midwest.

E. Lynn Miller, ASLA, is professor of landscape architecture at the Pennsylvania State University, University Park. He is a recipient of the Bradford Williams Award of the American Society of Landscape Architects for professional writing and is working on a biography of Charles Eliot.

Keith N. Morgan is assistant professor and director of graduate studies in art history at Boston University. He writes on 19th- and early 20th-century architecture and landscape history. His interest in

Charles Platt as an architect and landscape architect culminated in *Charles A. Platt: The Artist as Architect*.

Darrel G. Morrison, FASLA, is dean of the School of Environmental Design, University of Georgia, Athens. He is a nationally prominent authority on the restoration of prairies and other natural landscapes.

Lance M. Neckar is assistant professor of landscape architecture at the University of Minnesota, Minneapolis. In his historical writings he has concentrated on the development of landscape architecture and urban design in the period 1890–1920. Formerly a city planner, he also serves as a consultant to the State of Minnesota Capitol Area Architectural and Planning Board.

Miriam Easton Rutz, ASLA, is a landscape architect and faculty member at Michigan State University, Lansing. She teaches recreation design and the history of landscape architecture and is a design consultant on recreational projects. Recently she has made video productions on recreation and design for instructional and public television.

David Schuyler is associate professor and chairman of the American studies program at Franklin and Marshall College, Lancaster, Pa. Among his many works he is author of *The New Urban Landscape: The Redefinition of City Form in Nineteenth-Century America* and an editor of the Frederick Law Olmsted Papers.

Anne Whiston Spirn, ASLA, is professor and chairperson of landscape architecture at the University of Pennsylvania, Philadelphia. Her book *The Granite Garden: Urban Nature and Human Design* won the President's Award of Excellence from the American Society of Landscape Architects.

Paul D. Spreiregen, FAIA, a Washington, D.C.-based architect, planner and author, organized and managed the nationwide design competition for the Vietnam Veterans Memorial. His books include *Urban Design: The Architecture of Towns and Cities*, *Building a New Town: The Story of Finland's Garden City, Tapiola* (with Heikki von Hertzen), *Design Competitions* and *The Architecture of William Morgan*. In addition, he has edited the collected essays of Elbert Peets and of the Canadian planner Hans Blumenfeld.

Frederick R. Steiner, ASLA, is director of the Center for Built Environment Studies and associate professor of planning, School of Architecture and Planning, University of Colorado, Denver. Like Frank Waugh, he is interested in the design and planning of the rural landscape as well as in the influence of education in shaping the built environment.

David C. Streatfield is associate professor of landscape architecture at the University of Washington, Seattle. He has written extensively on the history of garden design in California and is currently working on a book on this subject.

William H. Tishler, ASLA, professor of landscape architecture at the University of Wisconsin, Madison, is active in numerous landscape and preservation organizations and has published and lectured widely. For his work in developing the Old World Wisconsin outdoor museum, he received awards from the American Society of Landscape Architects and the National Endowment for the Arts. He has done extensive research on vernacular buildings and landscapes and is writing a book on the rural architecture of Wisconsin's ethnic groups.

Wayne G. Tlusty, ASLA, is associate professor of landscape architecture and a specialist in the Cooperative Extension Service at the University of Wisconsin, Madison. He has specialized in activities related to visual resource management with an emphasis on forested landscapes.

Suzanne Louise Turner, ASLA, is associate professor of landscape architecture, Louisiana State University, Baton Rouge, and a preservation consultant. She has served as president of the Council of Educators in Landscape Architecture and the Alliance for Historic Landscape Preservation and is researching the history of the antebellum landscape in Louisiana.

Noël Dorsey Vernon, ASLA, is vice chairman of the National Committee on Historic Preservation, American Society of Landscape Architects, and chairman of the Department of Landscape Architecture, Ball State University, Muncie, Ind. She has written numerous articles on landscape architectural history and serves as reviews editor of *Landscape Journal.*

Further Reading

General Sources

Ciucci, Giorgio, Francesco Dal Co, Mario Manieri-Elia and Manfredo Tafuri. *The American City: From the Civil War to the New Deal.* 1973. Cambridge, Mass.: MIT Press, 1979.

Creese, Walter L. *The Crowning of the American Landscape: Eight Great Spaces and Their Buildings.* Princeton, N.J.: Princeton University Press, 1985.

Francis, Mark, Lisa Cashdan and Lynn Paxson. *Community Open Spaces: Greening Neighborhoods Through Community Action and Land Conservation.* Washington, D.C.: Island Press, 1984.

Greenbie, Barrie B. *Spaces: Dimensions of the Human Landscape.* New Haven, Conn.: Yale University Press, 1981.

Harris, Charles W., and Nicholas T. Dines. *Time-Savers Standards for Landscape Architecture: Design and Construction Data.* New York: McGraw-Hill, 1988.

Hough, Michael. *City Form and Natural Processes: Towards a New Urban Vernacular.* New York: Van Nostrand Reinhold, 1984.

Jellicoe, Geoffrey, and Susan Jellicoe. *The Landscape of Man: Shaping the Environment from Pre-history to the Present Day.* 1975. New York: Van Nostrand Reinhold, 1983.

Laurie, Michael. *Introduction to Landscape Architecture.* New York: American Elsevier, 1986.

Lynch, Kevin. *Site Planning.* Cambridge, Mass.: MIT Press, 1981.

McHarg, Ian. *Design with Nature.* Garden City, N.Y.: Doubleday, 1969.

Mann, William A. *Space and Time in Landscape Architectural History.* Washington, D.C.: Landscape Architecture Foundation, 1981.

Marshall, Lane. *Action by Design: Facilitating Design Decisions into the 21st Century.* Washington, D.C.: American Society of Landscape Architects, 1983.

Morrow, Baker H. *A Dictionary of Landscape Architecture.* Albuquerque: University of New Mexico Press, 1987.

Nairn, Ian. *The American Landscape.* New York: Random House, 1965.

Newton, Norman T. *Design on the Land: The Development of Landscape Architecture.* Cambridge, Mass.: Harvard University Press, Belknap Press, 1971.

Powell, Antoinette P. *Bibliography of Landscape Architecture, Environmental Design and Planning.* Phoenix: Oryx Press, 1987.

Simonds, John O. *Earthscape: A Manual of Environmental Planning.* New York: McGraw-Hill, 1978.

_____. *Landscape Architecture: A Manual of Site Planning and Design.* New York: McGraw-Hill, 1983.

Sutton, S. B., ed. *Civilizing American Cities: A Selection of Frederick Law Olmsted's Writings on City Landscape.* Cambridge, Mass.: MIT Press, 1971.

Vance, Mary. *Landscape Architecture: Monographs Published 1970–1984.* Monticello, Ill.: Vance Bibliographies, 1985.

Designers

Thomas Church

Church, Thomas D. *Your Private World: A Study of Intimate Gardens.* San Francisco: Chronicle Books, 1969.

_____, Grace Hall and Michael Laurie. *Gardens Are for People.* New York: McGraw-Hill, 1983.

Laurie, Michael. "The Gift of Thomas Church: With a Visionary Understanding of California's Climate and Clients, This Landscape Architect Created a Lasting Vernacular for Western Garden Design." *Horticulture*, September 1985.

Messenger, Pam-Anela. "Thomas D. Church: His Role in American Landscape Architecture." *Landscape Architecture*, March 1977.

Streatfield, David C. "Thomas Church and the California Garden, 1929–1950." In *Festschrift: A Collection of Essays on Architectural History.* Salem, Ore.: Northern Pacific Coast Chapter, Society of Architectural Historians, 1978.

H. W. S. Cleveland

Cleveland, H. W. S. *Landscape Architecture as Applied to the Wants of the West.* 1871. Reprint. Introduction by Roy Lubove. Pittsburgh: University of Pittsburgh Press, 1965.

Haglund, Karl. "Rural Tastes, Rectangular Ideas, and the Skirmishes of H. W. S. Cleveland." *Landscape Architecture*, January 1976.

Hubbard, Theodora Kimball. "H. W. S. Cleveland: An American Pioneer in Landscape Architecture and City Planning." *Landscape Architecture*, January 1930.

Tishler, William H. "Pioneering with Plans and Plants: H. W. S. Cleveland Brings Landscape Architecture to Wisconsin." In *Transactions of the Wisconsin Academy of Sciences, Arts and Letters.* Madison: Wisconsin Academy of Sciences, Arts and Letters, 1985.

_____, and Virginia Luckhardt. "H. W. S. Cleveland, Pioneer Landscape Architect to the Upper Midwest." *Minnesota History*, Fall 1985.

Volkman, Nancy J. "Landscape Architecture on the Prairie: The Work of H. W. S. Cleveland." *Kansas History*, Summer 1987.

Andrew Jackson Downing

Downing, Andrew Jackson. *The Architecture of Country Houses.* 1850. Reprint. Introduction by George B. Tatum. New York: Da Capo Press, 1968.

_____. *Rural Essays.* 2nd ed. 1854. Reprint. Introduction by George B. Tatum. New York: Da Capo Press, 1975.

_____. *A Treatise on the Theory and Practice of Landscape Gardening Adapted to North America.* 1841. Reprint. Little Compton, R.I.: Theophrastus, 1981.

Haley, Jacquetta M., ed. *Pleasure Grounds: Andrew Jackson Downing and Montgomery Place.* Tarrytown, N.Y.: Sleepy Hollow Press, 1988.

Charles Eliot

Eliot, Charles. *Vegetation and Forest Scenery of the Reservations.* Boston: Lamson, Wolffe and Company, 1897. (Published posthumously)

Eliot, Charles W. *Charles Eliot, Landscape Architect.* Boston: Houghton Mifflin, 1902.

Steward, Ian R. "Parks, Progressivism, and Planning." *Landscape Architecture*, April 1968.

Tishler, William H. "A Tree Grows in Boston." *Connection: Visual Arts at Harvard*, Summer 1967.

Beatrix Jones Farrand

Balmori, Diana, Diane Kostial McGuire and Eleanor M. McPeck. *Beatrix Farrand's American Landscapes: Her Gardens and Campuses*. Sagaponack, N.Y.: Sagapress, 1985.

McGuire, Diane Kostial, and Louis Fern, eds. *Beatrix Jones Farrand (1872–1959): Fifty Years of American Landscape Architecture*. Washington, D.C.: Dumbarton Oaks, Trustees for Harvard University, 1982.

McPeck, Eleanor M. "Beatrix Farrand." In *Notable American Women: The Modern Period. A Biographical Dictionary*, edited by Barbara Sicherman and Carol Hurd Green. Cambridge, Mass.: Harvard University Press, Belknap Press, 1980.

Whitehill, Walter Muir. *Dumbarton Oaks: The History of a Georgetown House and Garden, 1800 1966*. Cambridge, Mass.: Harvard University Press, Belknap Press, 1967.

Henry Vincent Hubbard

Hubbard, Henry V. *Our Cities To-Day and To-Morrow: A Survey of Planning and Zoning Progress in the United States*. Cambridge, Mass.: Harvard University Press, 1929.

_____. "Parks and Playgrounds: Their Requirements and Distribution as Elements in the City Plan." *Landscape Architecture*, July 1922.

_____, and Theodora Kimball Hubbard. *An Introduction to the Study of Landscape Design*. New York: Macmillan, 1917.

Williams, Bradford, et al. "Henry Vincent Hubbard: An Official Minute on His Professional Life and Work." *Landscape Architecture*, January 1948.

Thomas Jefferson

Baron, Robert C. *The Garden and Farm Books of Thomas Jefferson*. Golden, Colo.: Fulcrum, 1987.

Beiswanger, William L. "The Temple in the Garden: Thomas Jefferson's Vision of the Monticello Landscape." In *British and American Gardens in the Eighteenth Century*, edited by Robert P. Maccubbin and Peter Martin. Williamsburg, Va.: Colonial Williamsburg Foundation, 1984.

Berman, Eleanor D. *Thomas Jefferson Among the Arts*. New York: Philosophical Library, 1947.

Betts, William M. *Thomas Jefferson's Garden Book 1766–1824*. Philadelphia: American Philosophical Society, 1944.

Kimball, Fiske. *Thomas Jefferson, Architect*. 1916. Reprint. New York: Da Capo Press, 1968.

Nichols, Frederick D., and Ralph E. Griswold. *Thomas Jefferson, Landscape Architect*. Charlottesville: University Press of Virginia, 1977.

Jens Jensen

Eaton, Leonard K. *Landscape Artist in America: The Life and Work of Jens Jensen*. Chicago: University of Chicago Press, 1964.

Fulkerson, Mertha, and Ada Corson. *The Story of the Clearing*. Chicago: Coach House Press, 1972.

Jensen, Jens. *Siftings*. Chicago: Ralph Fletcher Seymour, 1939.

Telfer, Sid. *The Jens Jensen I Knew*. Ellison Bay, Wis.: Driftwood Farms Press, 1982.

Warren H. Manning

Buck, Diane M. "Olmsted's Lake Park." *Milwaukee History*, December 1982.

Garber, Randy, ed. *Built in Milwaukee: An Architectural View of the City.* Milwaukee: Department of City Development, 1981.

McFarland, J. Horace. "An American Garden." *Outlook*, October 1899.

Manning, Warren H. "The National Importance of the Hudson-Mohawk Thoroughfare and Objects in Its Landscape." *Journal of the American Institute of Architects*, April 1917.

Schermerhorn, Richard, Jr. "Landscape Architecture: Its Future." *Landscape Architecture*, July 1932.

"Warren H. Manning, Landscape Designer. A Tribute to a Pioneer in a New Profession." *Landscape Architecture*, April 1938.

Wilson, W. H. "J. Horace McFarland and the City Beautiful Movement." *Journal of Urban History*, May 1981.

John Nolen

Hancock, John. "John Nolen: The Background of a Pioneer Planner." *Journal of the American Institute of Planners*, November 1960.

_____. "What Is Fair Must Be Fit: Drawings and Plans by John Nolen, American City Planner." *Lotus International*, 1986.

Nolen, John. *New Towns for Old.* Boston: Marshall Jones, 1927.

_____. *Replanning Small Cities.* New York: B. W. Huebsch, 1912.

_____, and Henry Hubbard. *Parkways and Land Values.* Cambridge, Mass.: Harvard University Press, 1937.

Frederick Law Olmsted

Beveridge, Charles E. "Frederick Law Olmsted's Theory of Landscape Design." *Nineteenth Century*, Summer 1977.

_____, and David Schuyler, eds. *Creating Central Park, 1857–1861.* The Papers of Frederick Law Olmsted, edited by Charles McLaughlin and Charles E. Beveridge, vol. 2. Baltimore: Johns Hopkins University Press, 1982.

Fabos, Julius Gy., Gordon T. Milde and V. Michael Weinmayr. *Frederick Law Olmsted, Sr.: Founder of Landscape Architecture in America.* Amherst: University of Massachusetts Press, 1968.

Fein, Albert. *Frederick Law Olmsted and the American Environmental Tradition.* New York: Braziller, 1972.

Roper, Laura Wood. *FLO: A Biography of Frederick Law Olmsted.* Baltimore: Johns Hopkins University Press, 1973.

Stevenson, Elizabeth. *Park Maker: A Life of Frederick Law Olmsted.* New York: Macmillan, 1977.

Frederick Law Olmsted, Jr.

Beveridge, Charles E., et al. *The Master List of Design Projects of the Olmsted Firm: 1857–1950.* Boston: National Association for Olmsted Parks, 1987.

Gutheim, Frederick, and Wilcomb E. Washburn. *The Federal City: Plans and Realities.* Washington, D.C.: Smithsonian Institution Press, 1976.

Stern Robert A. M., ed. *The Anglo-American Suburb.* New York: St. Martin's, 1981.

John Charles Olmsted

Olmsted, John C. "The Boston Park System." Address at summer meeting of the American Society of Landscape Architects, July 7, 1905.

_____. "Classes of Parkways." Report of Olmsted Brothers on a Proposed Parkway System for Essex County, New Jersey, June 14, 1915. *Landscape Architecture*, October 1915.

_____. "The True Purpose of a Large Public Park." In *First Report of the American Park and Outdoor Art Association.* Louisville: American Park and Outdoor Art Association, 1897.

Pray, James Sturgis. "John C. Olmsted: A Minute on His Life and Service." *Landscape Architecture*, April 1922.

Elbert Peets

Hegemann, Werner, and Elbert Peets. *An American Vitruvius: An Architect's Handbook of Civic Art.* New York: Architectural Book Publishing, 1922.

Shillaber, Caroline. "Elbert Peets, Champion of Civic Form." *Landscape Architecture*, November–December 1982.

Spreiregen, Paul D., ed. *On the Art of Designing Cities: Selected Essays of Elbert Peets.* Cambridge, Mass.: MIT Press, 1968.

Charles A. Platt

Croly, Herbert. "The Architectural Works of Charles A. Platt." *Architectural Record*, March 1904.

Monograph of Works of Charles A. Platt. New York: Architectural Book Publishing, 1913.

Morgan, Keith N. *Charles A. Platt: The Artist as Architect.* Architectural History Foundation. Cambridge, Mass.: MIT Press, 1985.

Platt, Charles A. *Italian Gardens.* New York: Harper and Sons, 1894.

Ellen Biddle Shipman

Anderson, Dorothy May. *Women, Design and the Cambridge School.* West Lafayette, Ind.: PDA Publishers, 1980.

Rutz, Miriam Easton. "Landscapes and Gardens: Women Who Made a Difference." Proceedings from a symposium at Michigan State University, June 9–10, 1987.

Teutonico, Jean. "Ellen Shipman." In *Long Island Country Houses and Their Architects, 1860–1940.* Setauket, N.Y.: Society for the Preservation of Long Island Antiquities, 1988.

Tripp, A. F. "Lowthorpe School of Landscape Architecture, Gardening and Horticulture for Women." *Landscape Architecture*, October 1912.

Ossian Cole Simonds

Eldredge, Arthur G. "Making a Small Garden Look Large." *Garden Magazine*, February 1924.

Gelbloom, Mara. "Ossian Simonds: Prairie Spirit in Landscape Gardening." *Prairie School Review*, vol. 12, no. 2, 1975.

Miller, Wilhelm. "A Series of Outdoor Salons." *Country Life in America*, April 1914.

Simonds, Ossian Cole. "Design in Public Parks." *Park and Cemetery*, June 1909.

_____. *Landscape Gardening.* New York: Macmillan, 1920.

_____. "Nature as the Great Teacher in Landscape." *Landscape Architecture*, January 1932.

Albert Davis Taylor

Jewell, Linda. "Construction: Notes on A. D. Taylor." *Landscape Architecture*, March–April 1985.

"Some of the Work of A. D. Taylor, Landscape Architect and Town Planner, Cleveland, Ohio." In *Architect and Design.* Chicago: Architectural Catalog, 1937.

S(trong)., W(illiam). A. "Albert D. Taylor, July 8, 1883–January 8, 1951: A Biographical Minute." *Landscape Architecture*, April 1951.

Taylor, A. D. *Forest Hill Park: A Report on the Proposed Landscape Development.* Cleveland: Caxton Company, 1938.

_____. "Kingsford Heights: Some Problems of Design for Prefabricated Housing." *Pencil Points*, October 1942.

_____, with Gordon D. Cooper. *The Complete Garden.* Garden City, N.Y.: Garden City Publishing, 1921.

Calvert Vaux

"Calvert Vaux." *Harper's Weekly*, November 1895.

Francis, Dennis S. "Further Notes on Calvert Vaux, Landscape Architect." *Association for Preservation Technology Bulletin*, vol. 8, no. 3, 1976.

Sigle, John D. "Bibliography of the Life and Works of Calvert Vaux." In *American Association of Architectural Bibliographers' Papers*, vol. 5. Charlottesville: University Press of Virginia, 1968.

Vaux, Calvert. "American Architecture." *The Horticulturist*, vol. 8, 1853.

_____. *Villas and Cottages.* 1857. Reprint. New York: Dover, 1970.

Frank Albert Waugh

Steiner, Frederick R., and Kenneth R. Brooks. "Agricultural Education and Landscape Architecture." *Landscape Journal*, vol. 5, no. 1, 1986.

Waugh, Frank A. *Country Planning.* New York: Harcourt, Brace and Company, 1924.

_____. *Formal Design in Landscape Architecture.* New York: Orange Judd Company, 1927.

_____. *The Landscape Beautiful.* New York: Orange Judd Company, 1910.

_____. *Landscape Gardening.* New York: Orange Judd Company, 1899.

_____. *The Natural Style in Landscape Gardening.* Boston: R. G. Badger, 1917.

Jacob Weidenmann

Weidenmann, J. *American Garden Architecture.* Unpublished. Copy, with assembled drawings, in the Miriam and Ira D. Wallach Division of Art, Prints and Photographs, New York Public Library, New York City.

_____. *Modern Cemeteries: An Essay Upon the Improvement and Proper Management of Rural Cemeteries.* Chicago: Monumental Press, 1888.

Victorian Landscape Gardening: A Facsimile of Jacob Weidenmann's Beautifying Country Homes. Introduction by David Schuyler. Watkins Glen, N.Y.: American Life Foundation, 1978.

Places

Campuses

Dober, Richard P. "Campus Planning." In *Encyclopedia of Architecture.* New York: John Wiley and Sons, 1988.

McGuire, Diane Kostial. "Early Site Planning on the West Coast: Frederick Law Olmsted's Plan for the Stanford University." *Landscape Architecture*, January 1957.

Turner, Paul V. *Campus: An American Planning Tradition.* Cambridge, Mass.: MIT Press, 1984.

Cemeteries

Adams, Lloyd, III. "The Cemeteries of New Orleans." *New Orleans Preservation in Print*, April 1988.

Darnall, Margaretta J. "The American Cemetery as Picturesque Landscape: Bellefontaine Cemetery, St. Louis." *Winterthur Portfolio*, Winter 1983.

French, Stanley. "The Cemetery as Cultural Institution: The Establishment of Mount Auburn and the 'Rural Cemetery' Movement." In *Death in America*, edited by David E. Stannard. Philadelphia: University of Pennsylvania Press, 1975.

Linden-Ward, Blanche. "Putting the Past Under Grass: History as Death and Cemetery Commemoration." *Prospects*, 1985.

———. *Silent City on a Hill: Landscapes of Memory and Boston's Mount Auburn Cemetery.* Columbus: Ohio State University Press, 1988.

———, and Alan Ward. "Spring Grove: The Role of the Rural Cemetery in American Landscape Design." *Landscape Architecture*, September–October 1985.

Maney, Susan. "Cemeteries as Parks." *Newsletter of the Landmark Society of Western New York*, May–June 1988.

City Planning

Nolen, John. *City Planning*. New York: D. Appleton, 1916.

———. *New Ideals in the Planning of Cities, Towns, and Villages*. New York: American City Bureau, 1919.

Reps, John W. *The Making of Urban America: A History of City Planning in the United States*. Princeton, N.J.: Princeton University Press, 1965.

Robinson, Charles Mulford. *Modern Civic Art, or the City Made Beautiful*. 1903. Reprint. New York: Arno Press, 1970.

Scott, Mel. *American City Planning Since 1890*. Berkeley: University of California Press, 1969.

Country Estates

American Society of Landscape Architects. *Illustrations of Work of Members*. New York: Hayden Twiss, 1931–34.

Elwood, P. H. *American Landscape Architecture*. New York: Architectural Book Publishing, 1924.

Leighton, Ann. *American Gardens of the Nineteenth Century: "For Comfort and Affluence."* Amherst: University of Massachusetts Press, 1987.

Sclare, Liisa, and Donald Sclare. *Beaux Arts Estates*. New York: Viking Press, 1980.

Gardens

Bye, A. E. *Art into Landscape: Landscape into Art*. Mesa, Ariz.: PDA Publishers, 1983.

Douglas, William Lake. *Garden Design: History, Principles, Elements, Practice*. New York: Simon and Shuster, 1984.

Hanson, A. E. *An Arcadian Landscape: The California Gardens of A. E. Hanson, 1920–1932*. Los Angeles: Hennessey and Ingalls, 1985.

Herman, Ron, ed. *Landscape Design: New Wave in California*. Process: Architecture, no. 61. Tokyo: Process Architecture Publishing, August 1985.

Ichinowatari, Katsuhiko, ed. *Landscape Design: Works of Dan Kiley*. Process: Architecture, no. 31. Tokyo: Process Architecture Publishing, October 1982.

Moore, Charles W., William J. Mitchell and William Turnbull, Jr. *The Poetics of Gardens*. Cambridge, Mass.: MIT Press, 1988.

Ray, Mary Helen, and Robert P. Nicholls, eds. *The Traveler's Guide to American Gardens*. Chapel Hill: University of North Carolina Press, 1988.

Van Valkenburgh, Michael. *Built Landscapes: Gardens in the Northeast*. Brattleboro, Vt.: Brattleboro Museum and Art Center, 1984.

Historic Landscapes

Austin, Richard L., et al., eds. *The Yearbook of Landscape Architecture: Historic Preservation*. New York: Van Nostrand Reinhold, 1983.

Favretti, Rudy J., and Joy Putman Favretti. *Landscapes and Gardens for Historic Buildings*. Nashville: American Association for State and Local History, 1978.

Fitch, James Marston. *Historic Preservation: Curatorial Management of the Built World*. New York: McGraw-Hill, 1982.

Melnick, Robert Z. *Cultural Landscapes: Rural Historic Districts in the National Park System*. Washington, D.C.: U.S. Department of the Interior, 1984.

Special preservation issues. *Landscape Architecture*, May 1976, January 1981 and July–August 1987.

Stewart, John J. *Historic Landscapes and Gardens: Procedures for Restoration*. Technical Leaflet 80. Nashville: American Association for State and Local History, 1974.

Stipe, Robert E., ed. *New Directions in Rural Preservation*. Washington, D.C.: U.S. Department of the Interior, 1980.

Stokes, Samuel, with A. Elizabeth Watson et al. *Saving America's Countryside: A Guide to Rural Conservation*. National Trust for Historic Preservation. Baltimore: Johns Hopkins University Press, 1989.

Housing Environments

Chermayeff, Serge, and Christopher Alexander. *Community and Privacy*. Garden City, N.Y.: Doubleday, 1963.

Cooper-Marcus, Clare, and Wendy Sarkisian. *Housing as if People Mattered: Site Design Guidelines for Medium Density Family Housing*. Berkeley: University of California Press, 1987.

Corbett, Michael. *A Better Place to Live: New Designs for Tomorrow's Communities*. Emmaus, Pa.: Rodale Press, 1981.

Untermann, Richard. *Site Planning for Cluster Housing*. New York: Van Nostrand Reinhold, 1977.

Institutional and Corporate Landscapes

Koetter, Fred. "The Corporate Villa." In *Design Quarterly 135*. Cambridge, Mass.: MIT Press, 1987.

Marvin, Robert E., and James Paddock. "Corporate Headquarters Achieve Minimum Landscape Impact." *Landscape Architecture*, January 1979.

Mueller, William. "Medical Campuses: Challenge and Opportunities." *Landscape Architecture*, June 1983.

Landscape Planning

Fabos, Julius Gy. *Land Use Planning: From Global to Local Challenge*. New York: Chapman and Hall, 1985.

Lovejoy, Derek, ed. *Land Use and Landscape Planning*. 2nd ed. Glasgow, Scotland: Leonard Hill, Blackie Publishing Group, 1979.

Zube, Ervin H., Robert O. Brush and Julius Gy. Fabos. *Landscape Assessment: Values, Perceptions and Resources*. Stroudsburg, Pa.: Dowden, Hutchinson and Ross, 1975.

Landscape Scenery

Huth, Hans. *Nature and the American: Three Centuries of Changing Attitudes*. Berkeley: University of California Press, 1957.

Nassauer, Joan Iverson. *Caring for the Countryside*. Station Bulletin AD-SB-3017. Washington, D.C.: Soil Conservation Service, U.S. Department of Agriculture, 1986.

Shepard, Paul. *Man in the Landscape: A Historic View of the Esthetics of Nature*. New York: Alfred A. Knopf, 1967.

Smardon, Richard C., James F. Palmer and John P. Felleman, eds. *Foundations for Visual Project Analysis*. New York: John Wiley and Sons, 1986.

U.S. Forest Service. *Our National Landscape: A Conference on Applied Techniques for Analysis and Management of the Visual Resource*. General Technical Report PSW-35. Washington, D.C.: U.S. Government Printing Office, 1980.

Metropolitan Open Spaces

Chadwick, George F. *The Park and the Town: Public Landscapes in the 19th and 20th Centuries*. New York: Frederick A. Praeger, 1966.

Zaitzevsky, Cynthia. *Frederick Law Olmsted and the Boston Park System*. Cambridge, Mass.: Harvard University Press, Belknap Press, 1982.

National Forests

Baldwin, Donald M. *The Quiet Revolution*. Boulder, Colo.: Pruett Publishing, 1972.

Steen, Harold. *The U.S. Forest Service: A History*. Seattle: University of Washington Press, 1976.

Tweed, William C. *Recreation Site Planning and Improvements in the National Forests: 1891–1942*. Washington, D.C.: U.S. Department of Agriculture Forest Service, 1980.

National Parks

Everhart, William. *The National Park Service*. New York: Frederick R. Praeger, 1972.

Hartzog, George B., Jr. *Battling for the National Parks*. Mount Kisco, N.Y.: Moyer Bell, 1988.

Shankland, Robert. *Steve Mather of the National Parks*. New York: Alfred A. Knopf, 1951.

Tweed, William C., and Laura Soulliere Harrison. *Rustic Architecture and the National Parks: The History of a Design Ethic*. Lincoln: University of Nebraska Press, forthcoming.

Wirth, Conrad C. *Parks, Politics, and the People*. Norman: University of Oklahoma Press, 1980.

New Towns and Planned Communities

Alanen, Arnold R., and Joseph A. Eden. *Main Street Ready-Made: The New Deal Community of Greendale, Wisconsin*. Madison: State Historical Society of Wisconsin, 1987.

Breckenfeld, Gurney. *Columbia and the New Cities*. New York: Ives Washburn, 1971.

Garner, John S. *The Model Company Town: Urban Design Through Private Enterprise in Nineteenth-Century New England*. Amherst: University of Massachusetts Press, 1984.

Golany, Gideon, and Daniel Walden, eds. *The Contemporary New Communities Movement in the United States*. Urbana: University of Illinois Press, 1974.

Grubisich, Tom, and Peter McCandless. *Reston: The First Twenty Years*. Reston, Va.: Reston Publishing, 1985.

Howard, Ebenezer. *Garden Cities of To-morrow*. 1898. Reprint. Cambridge, Mass.: MIT Press, 1965.

Klaus, Susan L. *Links in the Chain: Greenbelt, Maryland, and the New Town Movement in America. An Annotated Bibliography on the Occasion of the Fiftieth Anniversary of Greenbelt, Maryland*. Washington Area Studies, no. 13. Washington, D.C.: George Washington University, 1987.

Stein, Clarence. *Toward New Towns for America*. Cambridge, Mass.: MIT Press, 1957.

Williamson, Mary Lou, ed. *Greenbelt: History of a New Town, 1937–1987*. Norfolk: Donning Company, 1987.

Parkways

Jolley, Harley. *Painting with a Comet's Tail*. Boone, N.C.: Appalachian Consortium Press, 1987.

U.S. Department of Commerce. *A Proposed Program for Scenic Roads and Parkways*. Washington, D.C.: U.S. Government Printing Office, 1965.

U.S. Department of the Interior. *National Parkways Handbook*. Washington, D.C.: U.S. Government Printing Office, 1964.

Westchester County Park Commission. *Report of the Westchester County Park Commission*. Bronxville, N.Y.: Author, 1924.

Recreational Areas

Epperson, Arlin F. *Private and Commercial Recreation*. New York: John Wiley and Sons, 1977.

Gunn, Claire A. *Vacationscape: Designing Tourist Regions*. Austin: Bureau of Business Research, University of Texas, 1972.

Hultsman, John, Richard L. Cottrell and Wendy Sales Hultsman. *Planning Parks for People*. State College, Pa.: Venture Publishing, 1987.

Knapp, Richard F., and Charles E. Hartsoe. *Play for America*. Alexandria, Va.: National Recreation and Park Association, 1979.

Molner, Donald J., and Albert J. Rutledge. *Anatomy of a Park: The Essentials of Recreation Area Planning and Design*. New York: McGraw-Hill, 1986.

U.S. Forest Service. "Ski Areas." In *National Forest Landscape Management*, vol. 2. Washington, D.C.: U.S. Government Printing Office, 1984.

Restored Natural Landscapes

Diekelmann, John, and Robert Schuster. *Natural Landscaping: Designing with Native Plant Communities*. New York: McGraw-Hill, 1982.

Hackett, Brian. *Planting Design*. New York: McGraw-Hill, 1979.

Hightshoe, Gary L. *Native Trees, Shrubs, and Vines for Urban and Rural America: A Planting Design Manual for Environmental Designers*. New York: Van Nostrand Reinhold, 1987.

Roberts, Edith A., and Elsa Rehmann. *American Plants for American Gardens*. New York: Macmillan, 1929.

Zube, Ervin. "The Advance of Ecology." *Landscape Architecture*, March–April 1986.

State Parks

Cutler, Phoebe. *The Public Landscape of the New Deal*. New Haven, Conn.: Yale University Press, 1985.

Myers, Phyllis. *State Grants for Parklands, 1965–1984: Lessons for a New Land and Water Conservation Fund*. Washington, D.C.: Conservation Foundation, 1987.

National Park Service. *Park and Recreation Structures*. 3 vols. Washington, D.C.: U.S. Government Printing Office, 1938.

Olmsted, Frederick Law, Jr. *Report of State Park Survey of California*. Sacramento, Calif.: State Printing Office, 1929.

Wisconsin State Parks Concessions Task Force. *1987 State Parks Revenue Survey*. Madison, Wis.: Bureau of Parks and Recreation, 1987.

Streetscapes, Squares and Plazas

Brambilla, Robert, and Gianni Longo. *For Pedestrians Only: Planning, Design, and Management of Traffic-Free Zones*. New York: Whitney Library of Design, 1977.

Halpern, Kenneth. *Downtown USA: Urban Design in Nine American Cities*. New York: Whitney Library of Design, 1978.

Morris, A. E. J. *History of Urban Form: Before the Industrial Revolution*. New York: John Wiley and Sons, 1979.

Trancik, Roger. *Finding Lost Space: Theories of Urban Design*. New York: Van Nostrand Reinhold, 1986.

Whyte, William H. *The Social Life of Small Urban Spaces*. Washington, D.C.: Conservation Foundation, 1980.

Zucker, Paul. *Town and Square: From the Agora to the Village Green*. New York: Columbia University Press, 1959.

Urban Parks

Clary, Raymond H. *The Making of Golden Gate Park: The Early Years, 1865–1906*. San Francisco: California Living Books, 1979.

Cranz, Galen. *The Politics of Park Design: A History of Urban Parks in America*. Cambridge, Mass.: MIT Press, 1982.

French, Jere Stuart. *Urban Green: City Parks of the Western World*. Dubuque, Iowa: Kendall-Hunt, 1973.

Heckschur, August. *Open Spaces: The Life of American Cities*. New York: Harper and Row, 1977.

Laredo, Victor, and Henry Hope Reed. *Central Park: A Photographic Guide*. New York: Dover, 1979.

Schuyler, David. *The New Urban Landscape: The Redefinition of City Form in Nineteenth-Century America*. Baltimore: Johns Hopkins University Press, 1986.

Spirn, Anne Whiston. *The Granite Garden: Urban Nature and Human Design*. New York: Basic Books, 1984.

Waterfronts

Clark, John, et al. *Small Seaports: Revitalization Through Conserving Heritage Resources*. Washington, D.C.: Conservation Foundation, 1979.

Clay, Grady. *Water and the Landscape: A Landscape Architecture Book*. New York: McGraw-Hill, 1979.

Cowey, Ann B., Robert Kaye, Richard O'Conner and Richard Rigby. *Improving Your Waterfront: A Practical Guide*. Washington, D.C.: National Oceanic and Atmospheric Administration, U.S. Department of Commerce, 1980.

Cullen, Gordon. *Townscape*. New York: Van Nostrand Reinhold, 1961.

Halprin, Lawrence. *Cities*. New York: Reinhold Publishing, 1963.

Harney, Andy Leon, ed. *Reviving the Urban Waterfront*. Washington, D.C.: Partners for Livable Places, 1979.

Litton, Burton R. *Water and Landscape: An Aesthetic Overview*. Port Washington, N.Y.: Water Information Center, 1974.

Mann, Roy. *Rivers in the City*. New York: Frederick R. Praeger, 1973.

Merrens, Roy. *Urban Waterfront Redevelopment in North America: An Annotated Bibliography*. Research Report no. 66. Toronto: University of Toronto–York University Joint Program in Transportation, 1980.

U.S. Department of the Interior. *Urban Waterfront Revitalization: The Role of Recreation and Heritage*. Washington, D.C.: Author, 1980.

Wrenn, Douglas M., John A. Casazza and J. Eric Smart. *Urban Waterfront Development*. Washington, D.C.: Urban Land Institute, 1983.

Journals

APT Bulletin
Association for Preservation Technology
P.O. Box 8178
Fredericksburg, Va. 22404

Garden Design
1733 Connecticut Avenue, N.W.
Washington, D.C. 20009

Garten + Landschaft
George D. W. Callwey, Publisher
Postfach 800409
Streitfeldstrasse 35
München 80
West Germany

Landscape
P.O. Box 7107
Berkeley, Calif. 94707

Landscape and Urban Planning
Elsevier Science Publishers BV
Journals Department
P.O. Box 211
1000 AE Amsterdam
The Netherlands

Landscape Architectural Review
24 Kensington Avenue
Willowdale, Ontario
M2M 1R6
Canada

Landscape Architecture
American Society of Landscape Architects
1733 Connecticut Avenue, N.W.
Washington, D.C. 20009

Landscape Australia
Landscape Publications
17 Carlyle Crescent
Mont Albert, Victoria 3127
Australia

Landscape Design
5a West Street
Reigate, Surrey RH2 9BL
England

Landscape Journal
General Division
University of Wisconsin Press
114 North Murray Street
Madison, Wis. 53715

Landscape Research
Landscape Research Group
10 Main Street
Cherry Burton
Beverly, North Humberside
HU17 7RF
England

Vernacular Architecture Forum Newsletter
P. O. Box 283
Annapolis, Md. 21401

Information Sources

The following organizations can provide further information on landscape architecture. Of special note is the Catalog of Landscape Records in the United States, which maintains a cumulative index to documentation for American landscapes and landscape architects past and present.

Alliance for Historic
Landscape Preservation
83 Wall Street
Suite 1101
New York, N.Y. 10005

American Association for
State and Local History
172 Second Avenue, North
Nashville, Tenn. 37201

American Society of
Landscape Architects
1733 Connecticut Avenue, N.W.
Washington, D.C. 20009

Catalog of Landscape Records
in the United States
Wave Hill
675 West 252nd Street
Bronx, N.Y. 10471

Dumbarton Oaks
Garden Library
1703 32nd Street, N.W.
Washington, D.C. 20007

Francis Loeb Library
Gund Hall
Harvard University
Cambridge, Mass. 02138

Frederick Law Olmsted
National Historic Site
99 Warren Street
Brookline, Mass. 02146

National Agricultural Library
U.S. Department of
Agriculture
10301 Baltimore Boulevard
Beltsville, Md. 20705

National Association for
Olmsted Parks
5010 Wisconsin Avenue, N.W.
Suite 308
Washington, D.C. 20016

National Park and Recreation
Association
1601 North Kent Street
Arlington, Va. 22209

National Register of
Historic Places
Register of Natural
Landmarks
National Park Service
U.S. Department of
the Interior
P.O. Box 37127
Washington, D.C. 20013-7127

National Trust for
Historic Preservation
1785 Massachusetts Avenue, N.W.
Washington, D.C. 20036

Society of Architectural
Historians
American Garden and
Landscape History Chapter
1232 Pine Street
Philadelphia, Pa. 19107

Thomas Jefferson Memorial
Foundation
P.O. Box 316
Charlottesville, Va. 22902

Index

Other Books from The Preservation Press

ARCHITECTS MAKE ZIG-ZAGS: LOOKING AT ARCHITECTURE FROM A TO Z. Drawings by Roxie Munro. An architectural ABC—whimsical illustrations paired with easy-to-understand definitions for architecture lovers young and old. 64 pp., 48 drawings, biblio. $8.95 pb.

INDUSTRIAL EYE: PHOTOGRAPHS BY JET LOWE FROM THE HISTORIC AMERICAN ENGINEERING RECORD. Introduction by David Weitzman. Features 120 color and duotone photographs of an industrial America that few people have seen. 128 pp., illus., biblio. $34.95 hb.

WHAT IT FEELS LIKE TO BE A BUILDING. Forrest Wilson. A delightful classic that introduces design and engineering principles to children age 7 and up through a sense of humor and clear, simple drawings. Brought back in a new revised edition. Landmark Reprint Series. 80 pp., illus., $15.95 hb, $10.95 pb.

Past-Age Postcard Series

DUCKS & DINERS: VIEWS FROM AMERICA'S PAST. Introduction by Chester H. Liebs. An array of pop architecture dotting the American roadside is captured on 24 full-color reproduction postcards, ready to mail. $6.95 pb.

PICTURE PALACES. Introduction by David Naylor. The glory days of nickelodeons and afternoons at the matinee are remembered through 24 full-color reproduction postcards, ready to mail. $6.95 pb.

Other Books

ALL ABOUT OLD BUILDINGS: THE WHOLE PRESERVATION CATALOG. Diane Maddex, Editor. This fact-filled book offers a lively, readable mixture of illustrations, sources of help, case histories, excerpts and quotations on 15 major subject areas. 436 pp., illus., biblio., index. $39.95 hb, $24.95 pb.

MASONRY: HOW TO CARE FOR OLD AND HISTORIC BRICK AND STONE. Mark London. How to repair and maintain old brick and stone in accordance with the Secretary of the Interior's Standards for Rehabilitation. Diagnosing problems, cleaning, repointing and strategies for correcting damage from moisture are all discussed. 208 pp., illus., biblio., index. $12.95 pb.

RESPECTFUL REHABILITATION: ANSWERS TO YOUR QUESTIONS ABOUT OLD BUILDINGS. National Park Service. A "Dear Abby" for old buildings, this handy, recently updated guide answers 150 of the most-asked questions about rehabilitating old houses and other historic buildings. 200 pp., illus., biblio., index. $12.95 pb.

THE AMERICAN MOSAIC: PRESERVING A NATION'S HERITAGE. Robert E. Stipe and Antoinette J. Lee, Editors. Thought-provoking essays examine the American preservation movement today. 336 pp., illus., append. Distributed for the U.S. Committee, International Council on Monuments and Sites (US/ICOMOS). $19.95 pb.

To order, send the total of the book prices (less 10 percent discount for National Trust members), plus $3 postage and handling, to: Mail Order, National Trust for Historic Preservation, 1600 H Street, N.W., Washington, D.C. 20006. Residents of California, Colorado, Washington, D.C., Illinois, Iowa, Louisiana, Maryland, Massachusetts, New York, Pennsylvania, South Carolina, Texas and Virginia, please add applicable sales tax. Make checks payable to the National Trust or provide your credit card number, expiration date, signature and telephone number.